The Vulnerable Generation

the
vulnerable
generation

elizabeth manners

COWARD, McCANN & GEOGHEGAN, INC.
NEW YORK

Contents

Author's Preface

This is a very personal book. I am not a professional writer; still less am I a professional psychologist, sociologist or educationalist. I do not claim to be expert in anything at all, certainly not in the bringing up of the young. I suppose I am a pragmatist; as far as I am concerned what works, works. For thirty years I have been a builder of bridges over the generation gap. They may be rather ramshackle and my techniques are probably out of date, but the odd thing is that the bridges seem to hold up, despite the winds of change and the tides of fashion. Not always, of course—for who can claim one hundred per cent success in so tricky an enterprise?—but, I like to think, more often than not.

If I thought that I was alone in believing that there is a crying need in the world today for a return to 'old-fashioned' concepts of discipline, responsibility and goodness, I should never have had the hardihood to write this book. It is because I believe, in all humility, that what I have to say is in the hearts and minds of millions of ordinary people, who lack the means to say it aloud but would like to hear it shouted from the house-tops, that I have taken my courage in one hand, the other being occupied with holding my pen, and put my thoughts down on paper.

I am resigned to being ridiculed by the trendy critics who reach for the vitriol at the very mention of the standards which I should like to see upheld and for whom *decent* is a pejorative word. I have not written this book for them and I am supremely uninterested in their opinions. If anything that I have said strengthens the will and hand of other patient builders and gives them fresh courage to continue laying stone on stone, however often the mockers and corrupters pull their bridges down, I shall be more than satisfied.

E.M.

Felixstowe,
May 1970.

Acknowledgements

I am grateful to all those who have given me permission to quote from their letters to me, and also to Miss M. D. Higginson, Professor C. A. Coulson and Sir Alec Clegg for permission to quote from their speeches.

The Vulnerable Generation

1

Small Beginnings

I suppose this book may be said to have been conceived, if not exactly born, when the President of Felixstowe Rotary Club turned to me and said, 'Perhaps I should have warned you that the Press is here.' I had just sat down after delivering what I imagined was a fairly harmless address* in which I had stated my views on discipline, with some incidental comments on the younger generation and those whom I regarded as their corrupters.

I thought my views relatively unsensational, since it was the third time that I had made that particular speech and, although it had been well received before, it had caused no noticeable flutter in the Felixstowe dovecotes. In fact, my main feeling was that it was high time I wrote another speech for such occasions, as I had probably exhausted my local audience, with the Round Table, the Inner Wheel (who had obviously told their husbands) and now the Rotarians. It occurred to me that I might just possibly make it do once more, for the Felixstowe Ladies' Circle, and then it really would have to be scrapped. I do not know if I even thought that it was a pity not to have made more impact. I certainly cared about my subject, and I was glad that my audiences, mainly of parents of teenage children, had received it well and apparently agreed with me. I hoped that something of what they had heard would remain with them, for, as I had said in my address, it is better to light one candle than to sit and grumble at the darkness. I remember thinking that that was rather a good phrase and wondering idly whether I had made it up or heard it from someone else! I could not have guessed how far that particular little candle was going to throw its beam.

Even when I knew that a reporter from the local paper was

*Readers who were unable to be present for the fairly harmless address will find it reprinted in full as the Appendix, p. 205.

present, I was unconcerned, for I had seen notices of Rotarian luncheon speeches often enough: one small paragraph with the speaker's name and a line or two about his subject. I might get a little more because I was a woman and Rotary rarely had women speakers. So I acknowledged the vote of thanks, gratefully drank another cup of coffee in place of the one which had grown cold while I talked, and soon afterwards drove back to College for the rest of a routine day in the spring term.

The first intimation that something unusual was happening was a telephone-call late at night from the *Daily Mirror*. I was so annoyed because the reporter had somehow found my unlisted telephone-number that I hardly noticed that he was quoting large parts of my speech and asking me to confirm that these were indeed my views. It soon became fairly obvious that, out of a speech of three thousand words, some dozen lines had been selected for comment. I tried to protest that taken out of context these lines distorted the whole of my address, but it was useless. I had to admit that, yes, I had said those things, though that was not exactly what I had *meant*. I got the distinct impression that words had been missed out or altered here and there and so my views were being made to sound much more violent and dogmatic than ever I had intended them to be; but, since I was actually in bed and certainly did not sleep with my deathless prose under my pillow, I had no way of checking the accuracy of what was being quoted to me, and my feeble protests went virtually unheeded. The *Mirror* rang off; I lay for some time wakeful and uneasy, then swallowed two aspirins, turned over and went to sleep.

And woke to find my name in every newspaper and my views, reported with varying degrees of inaccuracy, on nearly every breakfast table.

Not that I realized at first what had happened. No doubt because of broken sleep, I was late getting up and had no time even to glance at the newspaper or to listen to the B.B.C. before going in to morning school. There seemed to be more girls than usual crowding around the reading-desk on which *The Times* was displayed, but the significance still escaped me. If I had thought about the previous night's telephone-call, it would only have been to reflect that the college library did not subscribe to the *Mirror*. Under no conceivable circumstances could I imagine *The Times*'s being interested in what a middle-aged headmistress had said to a small, provincial branch of Rotary. Nor did my secretary's arrival, brandishing the local paper with its headline COLLEGE HEADMISTRESS LASHES THE PERMISSIVE SOCIETY, shake me out of my preoccupation with the morning mail. I glanced at the article, slightly surprised at its length, saw that, though necessarily cut, it was a pretty fair account of what I had tried to say the day before and put it aside.

A few minutes later, I took time off to read the headlines in *The Times* and was startled to see on the front page, TEEN-AGERS TOLD TO WORK OR STARVE. My main reaction was one of distress: with all due respect for the august *Times*, I felt that this was the *Mirror* all over again. Taken out of context, without the qualifying ifs and buts which make all the difference, my views seemed to me intolerant, illiberal, all the things I most disliked. I longed to redress the balance, to cry out that this was not *all* that I had said and that the really important things had been missed out. When I had recovered from the shock of finding myself on the front page of *The Times*, I realized that the report was actually fair enough, but only so far as it went.

And there was far worse to come. In the next half-hour, various members of staff came in with their morning papers, each with its lurid headline—HEAD HITS AT SLUSHY PRAISE FOR TEENAGERS, STUDENTS TOLD 'WORK OR STARVE', 'SLUSH' SAYS THE HEAD! When I was handed the *Express* with its HIDEOUS HORRIBLE TEEN-AGERS, BY MISS MANNERS, I was ready to weep with rage and frustration. Could I possibly dare to hope that the three hundred delightful young people of whom I had charge would know me and trust me enough to realize that I would never in a thousand years have said that? And what in Heaven's name would their parents think? Not to mention my Governors. For one panic-stricken moment I had visions of wholesale

3

withdrawals from College, of the sixth form sitting in or even marching in protest. Imagination boggled and, fortunately, common sense reasserted itself.

Nevertheless, when the telephone started to ring with B.B.C. T.V. and radio, I.T.V., and one newspaper after another all asking for interviews and a further elaboration of my views, I was relieved. Not that I felt that I should in any way enjoy the subsequent publicity. I had had enough of that to last me a lifetime when, a few years back, I had crossed swords with Authority on the subject of a botched-up plan for comprehensive schools, a conflict which had resulted in my leaving a maintained grammar school in Manchester for Felixstowe and an independent school. But I grasped thankfully at the opportunity of putting the record straight, of saying the things which mattered and which had been almost entirely ignored in favour of the more sensational headline-stealers—a perfect example of one of the things which I most deplored in the handling by the mass media of news about young people.

I was vastly relieved to be shown every courtesy by the feature writers and interviewers who crowded my study for the rest of that long and bewildering day. At one time, while I.T.V. were filming and recording inside my study, B.B.C. were setting up their cameras on the lawns outside and newspaper reporters were waiting in the hall. The only possible way to fit in an interview with a charming young man from, I think, the *Telegraph*, was to take him in to have lunch with the girls. I hope he enjoyed it. At least he had the opportunity of seeing that my youngsters do not exactly tremble at my lightest word. I have no very clear recollection of our conversation but I know that we all laughed a lot, which is a fairly normal state of affairs at meal-times. Incidentally, all the girls accepted the invasion of T.V. and newspaper men as though it were the most natural thing in the world, giving interviews and facing the cameras with far more self-possession than their harassed headmistress.

Some of the results of this day's hectic activity were highly entertaining. I particularly enjoyed the article beginning, *Our Head is no square, say the mini-skirt girls*, in which one anonymous and charitable child remarked of me, 'Miss Manners may not

4

like all our music but you should hear her humming "Wandering Star" when she thinks no one is listening.'

By five o'clock at night, when the last newsman had departed, I was completely bemused, dimly aware that there had been other newspapers on the telephone and that I had promised to call them back if I had time but that I had *not* had time, especially for one paper which wanted me to read aloud over the telephone the entire text of my speech so that they could make a centre-page spread of it and invite readers' comments. It was a relief to escape to the sanity of teaching French to a couple of junior forms. The complexities of the agreement of the past participle seemed simplicity itself after a day spent discussing the permissive society, and I found myself hoping that I should now be allowed to slide back into my quiet academic groove and get on with the job of bringing up my reasonably civilized three hundred without bothering any further about other people's problems.

I happened to have found that my particular way of dealing with the young worked, my 'discipline rooted and grounded in love', to quote one phrase from my Rotary speech which hardly anyone had thought worth mentioning, even though I had said it was the most important point which I had to make. This did not necessarily mean that other people would find it a viable method, and anyway, who was I to pontificate? What had begun as a friendly chat over lunch to friends and neighbours (for most of the Rotarians were known to me personally) had somehow been inflated far beyond its intrinsic importance, and I had an uncomfortable feeling that the general public, especially those with children of their own, would feel irritation and resentment at being castigated by an unmarried woman for 'licking the boots of the teenagers' and 'pouring out adulatory slush about the Young'. Several of the reporters had asked me outright whether I was not afraid of being branded an 'educational Mary Whitehouse'. These words were put into my mouth by interviewers, although I did not actually say them.

It was even suggested—and this was frankly frightening—that militant students from the local universities might stage a demo at the College. It was, after all, only a few days earlier that some of my sixth had visited the University of Essex, where they had been met by exponents of pupil-power who urged them to throw off the tyranny of their teachers. I shall have more to say of this particular encounter later. Suffice it for the moment that I was genuinely concerned, as were several members of staff, lest we should become the target for some militant action, even some 'aggro' from the local skinheads.

Moreover, as I went back to lock up my office for the night, I remembered that in 1967 I had been interviewed by the *Daily Mail* on a similar subject. It had not caused very much stir: four people had written to agree with me. But there had been one anonymous letter from 'a few of the younger geneation' (*sic*). Although illiterate and totally irrelevant, it had been expressed in terms of vicious personal abuse—'We all understand plainly why you are not married and also know that jealousy gets you know (*sic*) where.' Any normal human being prefers to be liked rather than otherwise, and I was not looking forward to receiving once again that sort of poisonpen effusion, even in the ratio of one unpleasant to four pleasant.

By now I was physically tired and emotionally exhausted by the day's events, and it was only a short step to depression and a fervent wish that I had kept my mouth shut and let the permissive society stew in its own nasty juice. It was therefore with considerable surprise that I read the messages left on my office desk by my secretaries whom I had not seen since the morning but who, it now appeared, had been answering the telephone pretty well continuously. To begin with, there were three telegrams of congratulations, one from the parents of a child in the school but the others from complete strangers. Then there was a note from my secretaries saying that they had lost count of the number of congratulatory telephone-calls. Tired but definitely comforted, I trudged off to my blessedly quiet house.

But the day was not yet ended. After watching myself on television and deciding not for the first time that I really should diet, I tried to settle with a book, only to be dragged to the telephone yet again to record an interview for *Late Night Extra* on B.B.C. 2. Several friends told me later that they had heard it.

I have no idea what time it was broadcast nor what I sounded like for I was fast asleep.

All this happened on Friday, 6 March. The next day, I arrived in College to find my secretary opening an enormous stack of letters, sixty-two in all. As ill luck would have it, the very first was frighteningly abusive. Let me say here and now that, in all, I have received only fifteen letters opposing my views and that some of them have been couched in reasonable terms. Unfortunately, that first one was much more typical of the opposition, and for that reason I shall quote it in full, for it sadly illustrates some of the youth of today, full of incoherent bitterness, violent and dangerous in their mindless hate of anyone who dares to disagree with them, apparently only able to spell one word: *Out!* Despite a good night's sleep, I felt infinitely depressed when I read the following (spelling and punctuation untouched):

Its about time people like yourself moved with the times. Do you honestly expect modern youth to remain stagnant. Our values good or bad were brought about by your generation, after all it was your generation that polluted the Earth, its your generation thats responsible for all the strife in the world today. From your article in the Newspaper its evident that your views are that of a RightWing snob, frigid and left on the shelf and that God knows how you hope to influence you Girls as you might call them with your antiquated views. I never had the proper opportunities and I dont grumble about it but i am jolly well pleased that our Student arent sitting back on there arses, contemplating a future weath without giving a dam about the Old, Infirm, poor, and hungry of this So Called free Country. And what on Earth do you mean by lickig boots, if you did that to me Ied spit in you face. You detestable, ugly orgue.

Yours Hatefully

P.S. WHAT YOU NEED, OR SHOULD I SAY NEEDED IS A MAN. OR PERHAPS A WOMEN?

Quite apart from the spelling and atrocious writing, this made a pretty depressing start to the day, but I steeled myself to read some of the others. To my utter amazement, all but one of the

7

rest applauded me in the warmest terms. The second letter in opposition was thoughtful and reasonably polite, written by two sixth-form boys, and—which I later found to be unusual amongst the opposition—conceded the possibility that I might have been incompletely reported in the newspapers and courteously asked for a fuller statement of my views.

The sixty letters of support ranged from a brisk 'Well done!' to very long, closely written screeds, often autobiographical and sometimes containing original verse. Many people sent me articles from newspapers or even pamphlets. What struck me as most remarkable was that they came from people in every conceivable walk of life and of every age, including many in their teens and early twenties. I read them with growing wonder that anything of mine should have aroused such passionate enthusiasm and greatly impressed by the constant repetition of one sentiment, however variously expressed. Six weeks later, the flood of letters had dwindled to a trickle, but they were still arriving by each post and still the message was the same: *Congratulations on expressing what the majority of responsible people in this country are thinking.*

At first, I genuinely hoped to answer every letter personally, but as the flood swelled each day and the postman was delivering them tied together in large bundles, I realized that this was impossible. I stopped counting when the total passed the six-hundred mark. I felt that even a circular letter would put a lot of extra work on my long-suffering secretaries (besides costing a small fortune in stamps), yet some reply was clearly needed, for so many letters asked extremely pertinent questions and all urged me to 'go on talking'. Again and again it was said: *No one listens to us but you are in a position to be heard when you speak.* This was not a point of view which would ever have occurred to me, and yet in view of the tremendous reaction to my innocent words to Rotary it seemed as though my correspondents were justified.

Their good wishes for my future were warm and sincere, though sometimes amusing. Many thought that I should be in Parliament, perhaps as Minister of Education, although at least one admirer added 'preferably as Prime Minister', and another thought that a Parliament composed entirely of women like me would be an excellent improvement! One thought I deserved a monument 'at least as high as Lord Nelson'.

But it was only when the letters began to arrive with foreign postmarks that I really felt that I had perhaps started something and should follow it up. I had been genuinely surprised to learn from the letters that I had been reported not only in the national dailies and Sunday papers but also in most local journals, as many people mentioned by name newspapers from different parts of the country. Six days after my original speech, the *Toronto Daily Star* was hailing me, somewhat improbably, as 'an unexpected British Joan of Arc' who had 'sounded the rallying call against teenage tyranny' and could well do 'for the golden teenage myth what Hans Andersen's small boy did for the emperor's new clothes—expose it as a big phoney'. This last comment I found interesting, as exactly the same point had been made in several letters from British correspondents, and it was an analogy which had occurred to me, without my ever having put it into words.

What I had said was this: that it is high time that those of us who refuse to be brainwashed into the belief that all truth, honour, nobility not to mention might, majesty, dominion and power lie in the under-twenties, stood up and said so, and that I was sick and tired of listening to the older generation 'pouring out adulatory slush' (the papers had a field day with that phrase) about the Young, who, we are told, are far, far better than ever we were at their age. It is no wonder that these teenage emperors have come to believe that they really *are* vested with all these attributes since so many sycophants are continually telling them so, and often for exactly the same reasons as did the shady characters in the fairy-tale—in order to sell them something worthless. The very real nakedness of the young is all too pitifully apparent when their bluff is called and they are obliged to state their beliefs in terms more literate than chants of 'Ho-Ho-Ho-Chi-Minh!' or dirgelike repetitions of 'We Shall Overcome'. This emerges very clearly in an analysis of the fifteen letters written by my opponents. What precisely—if such an adverb may justly be used of letters which, on the whole, were sadly rambling and lacking in coherence—did these young people have to say?

In the first place, every one of the fifteen accused me of attacking their entire generation and wasted a lot of time in impassioned defence of their taste in clothes, music, hair-styles, etcetera, only to spoil the argument completely by going on to condemn utterly the clothes, music, hair-styles, etcetera, of my generation. One young man, perhaps lacking in a sense of history, seemed to hold me personally responsible for the Royal Albert Hall, St Pancras Station and the Tango, while at the same time lumping together the discovery of 'penicillan' (*sic*) and the atom bomb amongst the evils invented by the over-fifties.

The fact that I was headmistress of a public school obviously aroused the fury of some of the fifteen. I was told with considerable heat that when schools like mine ceased to exist there would be no need for students to protest, an argument which I found a little fallacious in view of the violence of student militancy in countries where private schools have very little influence. Another young man assured me solemnly that in any school like mine 'pupils are regimented and sheltered and the homosexuality rate is high'. He *knew* this to be true because two of his relatives had attended such a school and had told him all about it.

All of them seemed stung by my reported suggestion that many teenagers could do with a good wash. This was immediately seized upon as implying that *all* teenagers were filthy, and my young correspondents wrote long and indignant defences of their own personal washing-habits, one clinching the argument with the somewhat mysterious statement that 'some sacred cows could do with a good wash too'. At least two seriously stated that young people were dirty because they could not afford hot water and soap and another that washing was harmful to the skin.

One and all, they assumed that I had been brought up in the lap of luxury and was 'absolutely devoid of any understanding of the difficulties that face the progressively-minded young adults in today's capitalist-orientated society'. Rather char-

mingly, though with smackable complacency and self-righteous-
ness, several of them told me 'that the comfort given by us to
the aged through the medium of Community Service Schemes
is worth all the fantastic developments of this century', happily
ignoring the fact that such schemes were originated and are
almost entirely administered, organized and financed by older
people. Yet another, on the same theme, attempted to justify
'change for the sake of change' as being in some mysterious way
that he did not make clear the duty of the young to 'the world's
oppressed and suffering'.

All accused me of being dogmatic and of generalizing. This
was perhaps forgivable since so many newspapers had reduced
what I had said to dogmatic generalizations. However, that did
not excuse *them* from writing pages of the most dogmatic
generalizations that I have ever read—and after half a lifetime
of marking homework, that is saying something.

I have no wish at all to mock these earnest young folk who
alone, out of the thousands who may be presumed to have read
and disagreed with my views, took the trouble to think about
them and to write to me, but I found the almost complete
intolerance, the illogicality and the incoherence of their thought
and expression infinitely depressing. The contrast between their
letters and those of the young who wrote agreeing with me was
immediately striking. Although my supporters seemed to come
from much the same background as my opponents, i.e., sixth
form and university, there was a tremendous difference even in
the lay-out and appearance of the letters. Writing, spelling,
grammar and syntax, quite apart from the relevance and logic
of what the writers had to say, were immensely better in the
letters of support than in those in opposition. I am not necessarily trying to prove anything with this—one cannot draw
valid conclusions in such an unscientific way—but I am making
the point for what it is worth. It was really very difficult to take
seriously letters which were anonymous, scurrilous, almost
illegible, or which, even when literate, put forward as a reasoned
and conclusive argument for dirt, clothes which I had castigated
as 'cheap and nasty rubbish', and general scruffiness, the fact
that such clothes were *not* cheap—one correspondent told me

how much he paid for his trousers!—and that 'a person's appearance is his own affair and simply reflects the character of the individual'. Exactly!

If the opposition depressed me in one way, simply because it was so pathetically muddled and misguided, it was, I suppose, encouraging to find what one had always suspected: that the so-called new and revolutionary views of the young were the same old stuff that their age-group has trotted out ever since the world began. The question seemed to be why it had suddenly become fashionable, even obligatory, to listen to these views as though they were proofs of Holy Writ. In fact, Holy Writ being rather at a discount with progressive thinkers, amongst whom one must no doubt number quite a few of our bishops, there are grounds for thinking that the Gospels according to Tariq Ali and Danny the Red should now be our bedside books rather than that square old stuff by Matthew, Mark, Luke and John.

A short time ago, during some troubles in London University, a letter appeared in *The Times*, signed by a number of moderate students, deploring the attitude of the militants who were demanding equal rights in every part of university life. These young people modestly suggested that they had insufficient knowledge and experience to make vital decisions which might affect the whole future of a great university and that, within certain reasonable limits, they were prepared to accept the authority of their teachers. One might perhaps have expected that some, at least, of those teachers would have been grateful for this eminently co-operative gesture on the part of their students. Not a bit of it! Within the next few days there was a letter signed by a professor (admittedly of a college of art, so perhaps he had a little more time for writing to newspapers than his colleagues in mathematics, physics, history, classics and other disciplines worthy of the name), which consisted of a scathing and vitriolic attack not on the militants who were seeking to wrest his professorial power from him but on these very moderates who had expressed themselves as satisfied that he should retain it. In most immoderate terms, he denounced them as spineless conformists without an original thought between them. Almost every pejorative phrase was there save only 'capitalist lackey' and 'fascist hyena'.

Perhaps, then, I am failing in my duty to the community in holding up for admiration rather than for scorn and ridicule the many young people whose enthusiastic letters of support raised my spirits from the depression caused by too much repetition of the thoughts of Chairman Mao. Who exactly were my young champions, and am I right in thinking that their views have at least as much right to be considered typical of their generation as those of the anonymous young man who gleefully told me that when I was dead and forgotten he would be refusing jobs to people with short hair?

In the first place, I received a tremendous volume of letters from parents of teenage children. Sometimes, the letters were actually signed by the children as well as by the parents, though more often the writers simply added that their children wanted to be associated with the contents. For example:

> You may be interested to hear that my teenager daughter who is very 'with it' entirely agrees with what you said and I've no doubt that a great many young people will take courage from your words.

Even more interesting were the letters from the young themselves, for the theme of all of them was: What a relief to find an adult who neither expects nor actively encourages us to behave badly! Again, I can do no better than to quote some examples.

> I know now that at least one person doesn't think that an unmarried girl of twenty-three is necessarily kinky. . . . I attended a very modern College of Education. On the Staff there were a number of persons who seemed to expect slightly eccentric behaviour and regarded this as the norm. The students who worked reasonably hard, did not sleep around and had no particular desire to radically change the structure of the college were considered odd. It was, in fact, only when I realized that I was happy in my 'oddity' that I began to settle down.

> I am nauseated by the way in which many of the older generation feverishly study the current hit parade. Do they really regard

mini-skirts and side-burns as the Elixir of Life or is it that they are afraid that the young will insist on euthanasia for all those looking over a certain age? Knowing that there are people like yourself among this frightened generation, I can continue to give them the respect that age deserves.

Finally from a Cambridge undergraduate, the Master of whose college wrote by the same post and in very similar terms:

> May I, as one of 'those teenagers' say how much I agree with your opinions. You say that you are sick and tired of the older generation pouring out 'adulatory slush' about the younger generation and their habits. So am I, and I believe a large number of young people are tired of the adulation that the young receive just because they are young. I too believe in 'firm loving guidance' of young people and in beneficial discipline, which acts as enormous security in the turmoil of a young person's life today. I hope that I am not so grossly over-confident in my own meagre abilities to discount help from older people with more knowledge and experience of the world than I.

This young man went on to raise a number of extremely thoughtful issues concerning the need for mutual tolerance to bridge the generation gap and for the proper encouragement of the social conscience of the young, points which I shall discuss more fully later.

These young men and women do not strike me as smug, priggish or in any way abnormal or even untypical of the vast majority of those of their contemporaries with whom I am constantly in contact. Yet when have we ever seen *their* faces on television or been given the chance to hear their views? And when some of them do seek to go on record as typical of the silent majority, as in the letter to *The Times*, they are attacked by one of their own professors. The hungry sheep look up and are not fed.

Next to the young, whose support was particularly precious to me, I welcomed the large number of parents who gave as their credentials, as it were, the fact that they were bringing up children in the way that they should go and apparently producing without too much difficulty happy, healthy, loving, reasonably obedient and yet lively-minded young people. Sometimes it was grandparents who wrote, vouching for three generations of happy families. ('The parents of 1 son, 3 daughters, and grandparents of 9 dear boys and girls.')

Perhaps the most thought-provoking letter of all read:

> May I add my support to your comments on the relationship between adults and children. I implore you to follow it up with as much publicity as possible. I'm sure countless parents would be grateful for your guide-lines. We know a very large circle of people and have lots of friends. Constantly we're being asked how we managed to 'cope' with our three children (a girl of 22 working for her Ph.D., twins of 17 working for A levels). Our answer is always the same—'We gave them our TIME'.

As I read these letters from parents, I was constantly struck by the fact that they, just like my young supporters, had gone almost without exception straight to the point of my remarks, which was the relationship between the generations, and had largely disregarded my quite trivial comments on hair, dress, dancing and so on, which were almost the only things which my opponents had seized on and attacked. The crucial issue of the responsibility of older people to the young seemed completely to have escaped my young critics. One might almost say that they were so blinded by their long hair and deafened by listening to pop music at a hundred and ten decibels that they could neither read nor hear my arguments.

Obviously, the letters which I was most pleased to receive, and to which I paid most attention, were those from the young themselves and from the parents and teachers who were apparently making a success of bringing up the young with 'discipline rooted and grounded in love'. It was very clear that my correspondents were neither saints nor sadists but just ordinary, simple folk who happened to believe in ordinary, simple *goodness*. One of my young critics wrote:

> What I am trying to get at, or rather express, is my annoyance at your presumptuous attitude that your feelings represent those of most of your contempories who are too kind or nice to express themselves; I believe you to be entirely wrong.

The extraordinary thing which emerged from the piles of letters was that, although I had nowhere made any such claim, had I done so, I should indeed have been entirely *right*.

I suppose that quite a number of letters were from fairly predictable people: professional men and women in teaching (from primary school Heads to a Fellow of All Souls, professors and lecturers in many kinds of higher education, many of them distinguished men with famous names); the law; the Services, both serving and retired; medicine from Harley Street to country G.P.s; architects; scientists—including some Fellows of the Royal Society; estate-agents; farmers; priests and nuns and ministers of various religions; wardens of students' Halls of Residence; youth leaders; superintendents of children's homes; Scout and Guide leaders; chartered accountants; managing directors; Chief Constables; industrialists.

Now, it would be only too easy to write off most of these categories as hidebound right-wingers, concerned only to uphold the Establishment. But this brings me to something else in which I passionately believe: namely, that those who by their blood, sweat, tears and sheer hard work, whether by hand or brain, have created our society have just as big a stake in it and just as much right to strive to preserve it as the iconoclast young, who have as yet done nothing for that society, have to try to destroy it. I therefore was in no way ashamed to find myself the spokesman for so many of the hard-working, thinking people of this country.

However, many letters were from much less predictable sources. I was, for instance, genuinely surprised to receive support from Commonwealth officials in this country, from the Dean of a famous American university over here on holiday, from the general manager of an international airline, and from a well known musician, but I suppose that these gentlemen too could be considered as tarred with the Establishment brush. Yet not even the writer who told me that I was a 'Right Wing snob' could entirely brush aside the member of a football team who wrote to me on behalf of the rest to say that they would 'take up a pint of the best and wish you the best'! Or the 'Ladies' and Gents' Hair Stylist' from Tadley, Hants. Or the middle-aged women who kept little shops in Stockport,

Cheshire and Burford, Oxfordshire. I especially liked a letter which ended: 'I hasten to add that I am not a crank but an ordinary secretary in the City of London.'

One of the most charming letters was from an old 'pro' who signed himself 'Clown Jimmi that was' and added that, at seventy-two, he was still learning. He enclosed two pieces of verse which I cannot resist including, one against what he called indecent youth and one for the decent, 'worthy of our kind thoughts and help'.

This Dose Age
This is the age of the psychopaths.
The frustrated ones, mismated ones,
The sheepdogs and kinks, scruffs and kitchen sinks,
Hippies, skinheads, mods and rockers,
A worthless herd of sods and mockers.
The moaners and the beefers,
Brave on pep pills, dope and reefers,
Singing spivs without a notion
Provoking exhibitionist emotion:
They know not where they go nor care,
This age of moaning youth in despair.

The second poem has no title.

Tis my belief, that on life's stage,
Star parts can be played by every age:
And we fading players of yesteryear
Must let youth play its part without a fear:
For no part of time can we e'er borrow,
As only time alone can say
If the efforts of our youth today
Have built a finer world tomorrow.

From R.A.F. Northolt came a letter whose writer had been most interested to hear my sentiments echoed and re-echoed by a remarkably varied cross-section of the large Service complement and general public attending an All-Ranks function that weekend. A coloured postcard of the osprey's eyrie at Loch Garten, complete with osprey, was sent me by a sixty-three-year-old factory worker who was still going to night school 'to get a little education because through economic circumstances I was thrown into a factory at 14 years'.

Which brings me to the last and perhaps almost the most important group of people who wrote to me: the pensioners, some retired professional people or widows of professional men, but many working-class people who had left 'elementary school' at fourteen with never a chance of the higher education which some of the young demand as a right and then despise when they get it. The bewilderment and genuine distress of these old folk was very disturbing. One spoke of a young couple who loudly complained because their neighbours were elderly. One old woman of seventy was still working because she could not live on her pension, her husband, gassed in 1916, having worked until four weeks before he died of lung cancer.

What clearly emerged from this group of letters was a deeply felt resentment of the fact that, in many cases, meagre pensions and fixed incomes were taxed and heavy rates were being paid to provide higher education for students who seemed to be totally irresponsible. Over and over again came the sentence: *The word* student *is fast becoming a very dirty word.*

My final quotation is from yet another pensioner, one of several who asked me not to divulge his name and address for fear of reprisals. His is a very remarkable and perceptive letter and I shall refer to it again. It says:

> This is due to upbringing as a lad my mother never sent me to school, poor as we were, with a dirty pair of shoes, hands, face, hair and clothes. If we were dirty we received the cane; if we were very disobedient in class we received it and when I look back I, like many of us O.A.P.s, do not regret that punishment as it made us into good citizens which I have passed on to my own four daughters and their children and we are proud of them and have earned their real love and affection which money cannot buy. I would like to add that we did not need drugs to make our brains to solve our education problems in school. If I did not like my job, I got another. I cannot tell my boss how to do it the same applies to the militant students etc. It is not fair to the conscientious and non-militant ones including the teachers so why not get the co-operation of the parents to your way of running the schools and colleges.

Why not indeed? But how? Obviously, there were very large numbers of deeply concerned people of all classes and ages who believed with me that *permissive* was not necessarily another word for *civilized*, as Roy Jenkins would have had us think. I did not exactly see myself as the Joan of Arc of the *Toronto Daily Star*, but I wholeheartedly agreed with them that it was time someone had a go at the teenage myth. If it were really true that my views were those of the majority, and those letters did provide some grounds for thinking so, then perhaps I ought to take the advice which so many of the writers urged upon me and go on talking. Or, better still, writing.

Only the tiniest minority of the letters could be said to have been written by the cranky or bigoted, either in religion or politics. True, there was one who sent me neo-fascist literature and another who wanted me to support Enoch Powell. Two letters were very long and full of Old Testament references which I have not yet had time to look up, but which I judge to be on the apocalyptic side. But my critics would certainly have been disappointed to find none of the hanging-and-flogging brigade (if indeed such people still exist) amongst my correspondents. What struck me as most astonishing was that so many people congratulated me, not only on what I had said but on my *courage* in saying it. This was the theme of many letters, particularly from men, who said with some shame that it 'took a woman to have the guts to say what had to be said'. Countless writers clearly expected that I would be deluged with letters of abuse, for they said that they were writing to reassure me. I had not thought that what I had said took any great courage, nor even that it required courage to discipline children, yet here again so many wrote of parents frightened of their children and begged me to go on giving a lead. One writer made three references to my 'courage' and said that, after living abroad for many years, she had returned to find England 'a sad, sad country and men sitting back doing nothing about it'.

So I decided to try to do something about it, and this book is that something. I feel lamentably conscious of my amateur status but am much encouraged by the gentleman from

Nottingham who wrote to the *Daily Telegraph* about me in the following terms:

> She has got what it takes. I am 50 years of age and I always say what I think and write it as well and if people don't like it they lump it.

Which perhaps is as good a way as any of writing this book.

2

All Our Future

I might have called this book *All Our Future*. The reference to the Newsom Report will not escape those connected with the education of the young, but lest there should be those who, quite understandably, cannot keep track of so many reports nor sort out Newsom, Plowden, Crowther, Robbins, Uncle Tom Donnison and all, let me remind my readers that the Newsom Commission were studying the education of average and below-average children whom they called collectively 'Half Our Future'. Whether we like it or not, we are bound to admit that the young man was right who vindictively told me that time was against me and that, when I was gone and long forgotten, he would be in a position of authority. Not half but *all* our future is, in the ultimate analysis, in the hands of the young of today.

If it be true that the generation gap is unbridgeable, that the young hate and despise us, that they are only waiting until they have the power, economic and political, to destroy us and our world, then that future may be a bleak one. Already, several novels have been written with the theme of teenage power, and it is a simple fact that in twenty or thirty years I and others of my generation will be old and comparatively helpless in a world governed by those who are young today. 'Clown Jimmi that was' is not perhaps the world's greatest poet, but the verses which I quoted have their point. What sort of people will hold our fate in their hands twenty years from now? Will they be Jimmi's 'Hippies, skinheads, mods and rockers' or shall we indeed find that 'the efforts of our youth today/Have built a finer world tomorrow'?

If one wanted to be an alarmist, one could point to the ritual murders which have recently shocked America, allegedly the work of young people, or even to the football hooliganism and the holiday disturbances in seaside resorts where, according to the chairman of one Magistrates' Court, 'there have been some gruesome, terrible offensive weapons' used. Mention was made of an air-rifle, a cycle-chain, bottles, a catapult and two-inch ball-bearings.

As far as one can ascertain, these weapons were used by one set of teenagers (skinheads) on another (greasers), but is it entirely science-fiction to envisage a time when two opposing sides might join forces against the common enemy—the older generation? The latest skinhead sport in London and others of our cities seems to be 'Paki-bashing'. Scrawled notices are seen on walls and in Underground stations—BASH A PAKI. Quite apart from any question of race hatred, one of the main attractions of 'bashing Pakis' seems to be that they are gentle, inoffensive people who do not hit back. What if the slogan should change and if these young thugs should take as their motto BASH A GRANNY? There used to be popular song in Scotland which began 'Ye canna push y'r Granny aff a bus'. If Pakistanis may be indiscriminately bashed for kicks, there seems no logical reason why, in the not too distant future, grannies should not be pushed not only off buses but under them. After all, it would cut down the bill for retirement pensions and leave more for students' grants.

Talking of grannies and buses, I cannot resist digressing at this point to quote from yet another of my correspondents, a woman of seventy-two who, with her eighty-four-year-old friend, was standing, laden with shopping, on a bus full of seated schoolchildren.

> I stared at a boy about 14 beside me; he sat tight, so I said to him:– 'If you don't buck up and get up and give me your seat, I'll pull you up by your ears!' He didn't wait for that, offered me his seat and I said a polite thank you and then other boys and girls offered their seats. Example is needed.

To return to my horror-comic view of a future where the old are at the mercy of the merciless young, it *is*, of course, pure science fiction. At least, one hopes that it is and that the recent film *The Devil's Touch*, 'a study in folk horror about a group of power-crazy teenagers behind a murderous witchcraft cult', really does refer to the seventeenth century and is not meant to symbolize what might be happening in the modern world. One at least of my correspondents clearly lives in considerable fear of the young, which in itself is a frightening thing. She is willing to be quoted but begs me, 'Not my name and address as unfortunately I am living amongst these students and living alone, they would assuredly take vengeance.'

Whether or not it is true that her student neighbours would 'take vengeance' is beside the point. This pensioner of sixty-nine like many other old people who wrote to me in similar vein, believes that they would and is afraid. This is condemnation enough. One thinks sadly of the youngster who reproved me for not giving him credit for 'the comfort given by us to the aged'. There seem to be quite a number of frightened old folk to whom the young have given precious little comfort.

What then is the truth behind the golden teenage myth? That something has happened, even in the last three years, seems abundantly clear, otherwise why should my article in March 1967, which got a good deal of publicity, have elicited only five letters in all, when virtually the same sentiments, almost exactly three years later, have caused such a stir? So many people have said that it is the first time ever that they have been moved to write to a total stranger. Perhaps the *Toronto Daily Star* hit the nail on the head when it said: 'Not so long ago this middleage rebel cry would have been hooted down. But it came at a moment when British students are in revolt (yet again) and when a popular law-and-order backlash is getting under way.'

It is useless to sneer and brush away this wrathful uprising of the middle-aged as the sort of thing which has happened in every generation from time immemorial. We are all familiar with the peevish quotations deploring the hair and manners of the young which a clever young journalist then reveals as having been written by Saint Bilius of Septicaemia in A.D. 230. We smile indulgently, admit it was a good leg-pull and agree with him that young people nowadays are absolutely no different from what they have ever been. A remarkably silly article appeared on the woman's page of the *Daily Mail*, saying that the charges which I had levelled against teenage music, dancing, clothes, hair-styles and cleanliness could be levelled at every generation, and going on to sneer at 'jolly Mums and Dads' launching off-key into 'Doggie in the Window', 'shuffling toe-crunching foxtrots', 'dowdy, expensive Sunday best' and 'butterfly-crimped perms'. (Incidentally, that last one defeats me for how do you crimp a butterfly?)

Generally speaking, those who hotly assert that youth today is either no worse or else very much better than it was in the Thirties and Forties have not the slightest idea what they are talking about, having almost certainly been born in the Fifties. Either that or they are those frightened people mentioned by one of my young correspondents who bolster up their own fast-fading youth by trying to be with it. No one with eyes, ears and a mind can fail to realize that there is a great deal going on among the young which is, whether better or worse, very *different* from what was happening even ten years ago. And the world before 1939 seems as remote as the planets.

Let us for a moment try to imagine someone, having been in a state of suspended animation since the Thirties, suddenly coming to his senses and taking a long, wondering look at the world of the teens and early twenties. Because he will find it difficult to communicate with the young, much of their vocabulary being a foreign language to him, he will probably have to rely on superficial impressions, on what he reads in newspapers and magazines and, most important, on what he sees on television. I cannot believe that he will be anything but gravely disturbed by what he sees, hears and reads.

We can disregard the impact of mini-skirts shorter than those worn by three-year-old children in the Thirties, though he might be forgiven for wondering why, when so many skirts barely cover the crotch, others are sweeping the mud from the streets and yet more flop untidily around the calves. He may, however, quite rightly disregard the vagaries of women's hemlines as irrelevant to a proper study of the age. What I think may trouble him will be the apparent invasion of Britain by Red Indians, for he will certainly see a number of figures of rather indeterminate sex dressed in fringed leather, headbands and an abundance of beads. Indeed, he may be forgiven for imagining that a high percentage of the young people on the streets are on the way to a fancy-dress ball, so little resemblance do many of their clothes bear to ordinary everyday wear. He will certainly have considerable difficulty in distinguishing the girls from the boys in this age of Unisex, and he will stare open-mouthed at the windows of Carnaby Street and the King's Road while at the same time wondering why girls and boys who can afford these expensive—because so quickly expendable—clothes apparently do their shopping at jumble-sales or second-hand shops. Despite the apparent variety of styles and the insistence on doing your own thing, Our Man from the Thirties will be struck by a depressing uniformity in the appearance of the young, the garishly coloured mini-dress, tights, and long straight hair—almost completely disguising the face and having to be perpetually shaken or twitched back—being just about as destructive of individuality as the navy-blue gym-tunic, black stockings and plaits of the Thirties.

Though he may find the fashions strange, there is no reason why Our Man should be shocked by them, but he will have every reason to be disturbed by the sheer dirtiness of a sizeable percentage of the young, and the general scruffiness of many more. He will remember from his boyhood having seen the very occasional tramp, smelly, bearded, with lank greasy hair down to his shoulders, shambling along in an old army greatcoat with dirty, sockless feet in broken, uncleaned shoes, with filthy trousers and collarless shirt. No doubt as a child he had felt sorry for such a man, thinking him a war victim, queer in the head from shell-shock. The men in the dole queues had not looked like that, for their threadbare clothes had been clean and their pinched faces shaven, their patched and broken boots polished till they shone. What then will he make of these products of the Affluent Society whom he sees looking exactly like the old tramp of his childhood, even down to the Army uniform? As for the derelicts hanging around Piccadilly or sleeping in the railway stations, the junkies waiting for their next fix, the drop-outs, the child runaways from home, he will have no idea what or who they are but will imagine either that unemployment has now reached crisis proportions or that we have a refugee problem.

Reading the newspapers and watching the television news will be a pretty traumatic experience for him. For instance, he will have seen students in Harvard and in Berkeley, California, and in Amman, Jordan, in screaming mobs, burning and smashing in an orgy of destruction. He will have read of the Essex students who have been sent to Borstal for trying to burn down a branch of Barclays Bank as a protest against apartheid, and of the seventy Labour M.P.s who have tabled a motion condemning the Liverpool University authorities for sending down one student found guilty of grossly disruptive behaviour. No doubt he will have been as puzzled as I am by a letter from the Bishop of Whitby 'explaining' that the conduct of the said student was the result of his having been 'driven to desperation by the authorities'. At the same time, he may have wondered why a military junta in Greece should cause Cambridge undergraduates to smash their way into an English hotel, overturning tables and food and terrifying diners.

But not all these accounts of unacademic violence can possibly have prepared him for the shock of reading on the same day that the invigilator of examinations in Mainpuri, India, has been hacked to death with knives by students whom he caught cheating. He will surely have been distressed to read of a thirteen-year-old boy being convicted of possessing cannabis resin, once he has asked someone to tell him what cannabis is, for it is unlikely that Our Man knew of it in the Thirties. He probably will ask his informant to explain why the late Labour M.P. for Bedford wanted advice on contraception to be given in the schools, and one can imagine his reaction on being told of the growing number of schoolgirl pregnancies, of teenage venereal disease, even of the girl of fifteen who has already had two abortions.

He will finally decide that he has read enough when he learns of the Education (Miscellaneous Provisions) Bill which has had its second reading in the House of Lords and which, he will gather, enables students, after a jolly day of burning and rioting, to return home to the mistress and kiddies, secure in the knowledge that the Welfare State will continue to pay them a supplementary grant wherewith to keep the home fires burning.

Turning for relaxation to the television, his mind boggling at the picture of dirt, disease, destruction, drugs and despair which all that he has seen and read has conjured up, whatever will the poor man make of *Top of the Pops*? Watching the apparently lunatic twitchings and shakings of the young people, each one outdoing the other in the eccentricity of their clothes (and the B.B.C. giving a prize to the weirdest), he may be forgiven for thinking that they are all under the influence of pot, L.S.D., French blues, brown bombers, horse, all these new and bewildering things of which he has just heard and to which, he has been told, increasing numbers of young people in their teens are becoming addicted. Some of the tunes he will find soothing and pleasant, not unlike the dreamy blues of his peaceful boyhood, and the singers, though long-haired to a man, will strike him as clean and tidy, even though their performances no doubt seem pitifully amateur to an ear accustomed to the voices and big-band sounds of the Thirties.

But I think he will switch off in fright and despair on seeing the rapturous acclaim given by the young audience (and their not-so-young disc-jockey) to a bedlam creature in a costume of satin rags, with matted tufts of long hair standing out two feet from his head and his face totally obscured by more hair, seemingly growing all over it. Try as he may, Our Man will only be able to distinguish one word of the shouted lyric and, since this sounds like the name of a prehistoric animal, he will not make much sense out of it. Perhaps, he may think wildly, this person is meant to be a caveman. Was there not once an entertainer called the Wild Man from Borneo? Could this be he or a reincarnation? When the act finishes with the 'wild man' grovelling on the floor looking as though he were trying to rape his guitar, Our Man has had enough and probably begs to be allowed to resume his interrupted trance.

I hope that I hardly need say that this is an unfair picture of the young people of the Seventies, but the plain and uncomfortable fact remains that it is not in any way exaggerated. Everything which our mythical man saw or heard, I have seen or

27

heard since I began writing this book, in the newspapers, on T.V. or in the streets of London. We do the young a grave disservice when we abdicate from judgement, and it is sheer idiocy to pretend that there is no problem and that we were just the same at their age. *We were not*, and God alone knows what would have happened to this nation if we had been. In the first place, most of their generation would never have been born, or if they had, it would have been to a life of slave-labour under the Nazi jackboot. What is the use of telling the young how brave and free and splendid they are with heroin addiction, venereal disease, illegitimacy and abortion rising with every day that passes? And unpleasant though the facts of life in this country may be, they are infinitely worse in America, where the criminal with the worst record of arrest is fifteen years old and a twelve-year-old recently died of an overdose of heroin, where children stagger home from school as high as kites on amphetamines or pot, where the city streets are not safe because of young addicts, desperate for money to support their habit, and where the student riots and the protest demos make ours look like the Teddy Bears' picnic.

So many parents of young children are terribly afraid of the future. Unsure of themselves and of the values which they represent, they dread their children's growing up and being absorbed into this frightening pop sub-culture, this tribal society which they fear and do not understand. This again was a recurring theme in the letters written to me, and it was sad to hear from parents who were actually apprehensive because their sons and daughters were showing signs of being sufficiently intelligent to get a university place!

If there were nothing more to be said of the younger generation than this, then one might be forgiven for quoting the old shepherd in *The Winter's Tale* who cried: 'I would there were no age between ten and three-and-twenty, or that youth would sleep out the rest; for there is nothing in the between but getting wenches with child, wronging the ancientry, stealing, fighting.' Fortunately for us, this jaundiced view of the young is almost certainly less true nowadays than it was in Shakespeare's day, when it probably gave a very one-sided picture. It cannot be too strongly emphasized that the vast majority of young people have immense potentiality for good and, in many ways, are the most important assets of our society. I am convinced that this is true, not only of the rather self-consciously aware young people who wrote to me smugly of all that their generation was doing for the needy and the old, but of the young of every kind of social background and of all levels of ability.

It is a fact of the very greatest significance that, over the last thirty years, the demand of the young for formal education has continuously outstripped the opportunities provided so that the bill for education has risen year by year and looks like continuing to do so for a long time to come. Every year since the end of the war, the numbers of children staying on at school after they could legally leave have risen and show no sign of decreasing. It has even been said that it hardly matters whether or not we increase the school-leaving age to sixteen, for so many youngsters are, of their own free will, continuing their education until and even after that age. This is particularly true of the intellectually able, and grammar-school sixth forms have trebled and quadrupled in size over the years, but every secondary modern knows too that increasing numbers of its pupils are unwilling to leave at fifteen and are even prepared, when given the chance, to transfer to the sixth of the local grammar school or else to a college of further education in order to obtain higher qualifications.

It has been claimed that this demand for more education is the fruit of comprehensive reorganization, but this claim completely ignores the fact that every school for many years now has been experiencing the same thing and that, for instance, a city such as Manchester, which has always made G.C.E. courses available in all its schools and facilitated the transfer of pupils between different types of schools, had long before comprehensivization been making excellent provision for large numbers of youngsters over the legal school-leaving age.

Although there is little doubt that the enormous expansion taking place in the universities is one of the causes for the present student discontents, nevertheless there surely can be no one so entrenched in prejudice as to disapprove of this expansion.

The fact that so many more young people are asking for and getting higher education is undoubtedly one of the most encouraging things that is happening today.

It is sometimes argued that, although children are staying in full-time education in larger numbers and for a longer time, the actual standard of the education which they receive is falling. 'Proof' of this is sometimes furnished by employers who complain that the intelligence of the average clerk, apprentice, shop assistant, etcetera, is manifestly lower than it was before the war. What these pessimists do not realize is that the boy and girl who, before the war, went into this type of employment would nowadays almost certainly get G.C.E. at 'O' level and quite probably at 'A' level and would then go on to some form of higher education and an entirely different kind of job. For instance, thousands of young people who in the Thirties only went for two years to a teachers' training college today go to university to take a degree in three or four years, and many more, who would have left school at fourteen for fairly routine jobs, now stay until eighteen and then go to colleges of higher education, so qualifying for the professions. It is quite possibly true that the general standard of intelligence, though not necessarily of education, of young people going into blind-alley jobs *is* lower than it was, but this is because so many more are qualified for better jobs than these. There is indeed a shortage of bright boys queuing up to run errands or to deliver meat or newspapers and of bright girls to go into domestic service or serve in shops, and a very good thing too, but this is because the young are demanding and getting more and better education, not the reverse.

If it is possible (and I have shown that it is) to paint a very depressing picture of youth obsessed with trivial and often evil things, from pop to pot, it cannot be ignored that, at the same time, more and more teenagers are taking advantage of opportunities not only for formal education but also for acquiring knowledge and experience of every kind. The very fact that there are part-time jobs to be had for the asking means that boys and girls of every social class look for holiday work as a matter of course. Naturally, the main attraction is probably the pay-packet, but in quite a few cases the work done is either voluntary or poorly paid, and it is the actual work experience which provides the reward, the feeling of doing something reasonably adult and of making a worth-while contribution to society.

Not by any means all of the young think, as they are often accused of thinking, that the world owes them a living. (When the Education [Miscellaneous Provisions] Bill which so amazed Our Man from the Thirties was being debated in the Lords, it was Viscount Massereene and Ferrard who said that he had heard of people who thought that the world owed them a living but this was the first time he had ever heard the world also owed them mistresses!) Very conscious that their continuance at school and at the university is a drain on their parents' pockets, boys and girls frequently spend long hours at rather dull jobs in the intervals of working for examinations, simply in order to be able to pay for their own clothes and provide their own pocket-money. Although canning peas, clerking in a mail-order store or serving in Woolworth's are not in themselves particularly valuable experiences, one can only applaud the determination with which many of the young carry out these chores on Saturdays and in their holidays, and I feel that it is an excellent thing that those who are eventually to secure the well-paid and more interesting jobs should have first-hand experience of what other, less fortunate people have to do all their lives.

It may very well be that the relative classlessness of today's young springs in some part from this kind of work experience. In a pre-war world where there were two million unemployed, no such opportunities existed, and it would have been quite unthinkable that undergraduates and sixth-formers from grammar and public schools, the future white-collar professionals, could work at menial jobs alongside the traditionally 'working class'. I may be forgiven for being a little cynical about the two students who advertised thus in *The Times*: *Two male degree students 19 years seek employment abroad preferable Mediterranean, mid-June to mid-September.* One wonders when they intend doing any studying for their degrees if almost the whole of the

Long Vacation is to be spent abroad—and, of course, they prefer the Mediterranean! But perhaps I misjudge them.

However, directories are published yearly listing no fewer than 30,000 summer jobs in Britain and another 30,000 abroad, most of which will be filled by enterprising young folk from our schools and colleges. From my own experience, I could give a long list of jobs well worth doing and, at the same time, providing matchless experience of the world outside school which girls in their first year at university have found for themselves and proceeded to do with superb self-confidence and efficiency. I think of one who went to the Lebanon as mother's help to a couple with a family of very young children, and of the two who spent three months in Canada working as counsellors at summer camps. Even to reach the camp at which they were employed was an adventure for girls only a few months out of boarding-school, for, after air and rail travel, they finally arrived at their destination by canoe. How interesting it would have been if a T.V. team could have interviewed these girls on their return or even visited the camp to see them at work, teaching small children to swim, to play tennis, to live under canvas.

In every university there are posters advertising the COMEX expeditions abroad, but the only time that the mass media pay any attention to COMEX is when an unfortunate young driver of one of their buses happens to be involved in a fatal accident. All over the world, young people, most of them students, spend most of their vacations in back-breaking manual work for little more than food and lodging: getting in the harvest, working on all kinds of construction, helping in a thousand ways in under-developed countries. It would be a refreshing change if the cameras could occasionally be trained on these students instead of on the lunatic fringe who recently interrupted a lecture by the Vice-Chancellor of Sussex University by thumping on his rostrum and shouting, 'You satisfy our demands and we'll let you carry on with the lecture.' The lecture, incidentally, was on the singularly non-inflammatory subject of the 1870 Education Act.

There is hardly a senior school in the country which has not some kind of voluntary service organized, and indeed, in some districts, the supply of volunteers, eager to help old people, the blind, the disabled, with their shopping, gardening, cleaning, decorating, exceeds the demand. There is no limit to the hard work that the young will devote to their freely chosen causes, and, even though they expect neither payment nor recognition, it would be rather nice if they occasionally got the latter.

The number of children born in refugee camps in Europe is now mercifully small, but I wonder how many of those who dismiss the whole younger generation as useless layabouts know of the large numbers of such children who were enabled to come to this country and be kept and educated through the money collected by our own schools? In eight years, the girls of one school with which I was associated sponsored three such children, not only providing the necessary money but also befriending them once they came to this country. How many blind people would still be groping in darkness were it not for the guide-dogs provided by the efforts of children? If I were to list the charitable work done in one year by the girls of my own school, I should be accused of self-glorification. Not only the activities already listed but also the painstaking making of clothes and toys for needy children, the selling of flags whenever approached by a charity for volunteers, sponsored walks and swims for the homeless (one thousand pounds raised for *Shelter* in less than a year).

I should not mention these things at all if I thought that my school was in any way remarkable. It is simply because I know it to be absolutely typical of schools all over the country, and probably all over the civilized world, that I use it as an example.

Despite the accusation that we are fast becoming a nation of telly-watchers, more young people than ever are involved in hobbies of one kind and another, many of them much more active and exciting than the restricted range of interests of previous generations. A glance at any school magazine reveals a multiplicity of societies and sports quite unknown to children in the Thirties. Whereas pupils before the war were considered lucky to be able to play hockey or football with a bit of tennis, cricket and just possibly swimming in the summer, today one finds a maintained secondary school challenging Eton in the

33

Hickstead horse trials and girls from similar schools travelling the world with the British fencing team. Judo, squash, skiing, golf, skating, sailing and canoeing, rock-climbing, gliding—all these and more are taken in their stride by the schoolchildren of the Seventies, while at the same time the more traditional team games still flourish and Wembley Stadium is packed to capacity by wildly excited girls, not for the Beatles or the Rolling Stones but for an international hockey match. There is probably more serious music-making and drama by the young than ever before. I know of one school where more than two-thirds of the pupils learn to play a musical instrument and of another where there is a waiting-list to join the school choirs.

Which is the true picture of our young people? Are they nothing but a set of weird tripsters, high on the arrogance of knowledge without wisdom, demanding rights without responsibility, an alienated sub-culture rejecting the values of our society and the rules of civilized debate, full of self-pity and secondhand rhetoric, a primitive, dangerous, tribal society with its own language, customs, dress, even its war-paint and ritual dances, inexorable in its opposition to everything its elders hold dear, childish, destructive, hell-bent on a collision course with authority, a course which can only lead to a fatal polarization with the young and the old glaring at each other in mutual hatred, misunderstanding and mistrust over the yawning chasm of the generation gap?

Or are they indeed, as young people should be, eager for experiment and adventure, critical yet compassionate, hard-working in the right causes as well as on their own behalf, thoughtful, and realistic in outlook, friendly and responsive, their quality, as I have already said, one of the most important assets of our society?

I firmly and sincerely believe the latter picture is the true one: that the great majority of them, *despite the folly of their elders*, are charming and decent young people of whom any society can justly be proud. If I did not believe this and if I did not so thoroughly enjoy associating with them, not least for their spirit of service and helpfulness as well as for their natural friendliness which overcomes barriers of age, class, nationality and race, then I should have changed my profession many years ago. I do *not* believe it to be true—and I should think that by now I have made this abundantly clear—that the young should be envied and adored simply because they are young. Having been young, I can see more disadvantages than advantages in the state. Neither do I believe, because my generation has provided the young with better education and better opportunities in every way than those which we had at their age, that they are therefore superior to us in every way, mental, physical, emotional and moral. After half a lifetime of dealing with them, I am far from convinced that the majority are very much different from what we were. Under the veneer of self-assurance they are basically as uncertain and vulnerable as young people have been in any and every generation, as easily pushed off balance and always more sinned against than sinning.

This may seem in direct contradiction of my apparently dogmatic earlier statement that we were *not* the same at their age as the young of today, and that there is, in fact, a great deal going on among the young which is very different from what happened in our time. The point that I am making as forcibly as I can is this: there is very grave cause for concern about a *minority* of young people and every reason for profound satisfaction with the large majority, who are probably only better than we were to the same extent as we were better than our parents and they than theirs, right back to the dawn of time. I happen to believe that, despite certain appearances, the world has been getting better for a very long time and that, barring accidents, it will probably continue to do so. It follows then that each succeeding generation is a slight improvement on the last, and that the younger generation is never as good as it thinks it is nor as bad as its parents believe it to be.

It may be wondered why, if this is my optimistic view of the world in general and of the young in particular, I am bothering to write this book at all, and why I ever launched my attack on the supporters of the permissive society. Simply this: although the less desirable elements in the younger generation are in the minority, they exercise an influence far in excess of their numbers and for all kinds of reasons receive an inordinate

35

amount of publicity. Their potential for evil is therefore very considerable indeed, and it is not beyond the realms of possibility that, in time, the normal majority might be infected by the abnormal few.

Every parent and teacher knows to his cost how disastrous the bad influence of even one child can be in school or home, how easily one rotten apple can spoil a whole barrel, how quickly an infection can ravage a whole community. We may look at our sons and daughters and the children in our schools and say with Shakespeare's Miranda: 'O brave new world, that hath such people in't!' Yet it is useless to close our eyes to hippies, drug-addicts, teenage unmarried mothers and bomb-throwing student activists, and hope that when we open them they will have gone away. It was Shakespeare's student prince who said, less naïvely than Miranda: 'Something is rotten in the state of Denmark.' Anyone who cares about the young must see that this should be said about the teenage world. The effects of the disease are clear enough and tragic enough. What we must do is try to find the cause and, if possible, seek a cure, before more twelve-year-olds die of an overdose of heroin, more little girls experience the degrading nightmare of abortion and more schoolboys sneak shamefacedly into venereal clinics or—and I am not sure which is the sadder—swagger brazenly into chemists' for contraceptives.

> The young have their good points in abundance but we cannot deceive ourselves and them for ever by ignoring their bad ones. For some time now, responsible parents have suffered from a conspiracy of hypocritical fawning over the young, they have been blackmailed by tendentious spokesmen of the communications media who have made it fashionable to pay a fulsome lip-service to young people.

Those are not my words but those of one of the many who wrote to deplore with me the boot-licking of youth by those who should know better. If we are ever to see in the world today the full development of what I have called the most important assets of our society, then we must take a long hard look at that world and see just what threats there are to such development.

3

The Golden Teenage Myth

Our values, good or bad, were brought about by your generation. The
fact that the amiable young man who voiced this criticism
added that he wanted to spit in my face should not, I feel, affect
my judgement when I consider the truth or otherwise of what
he had to say. That teenagers are made and not born is a self-
evident fact. Why is it then that almost overnight, it seems,
hitherto docile children appear to sprout horns and tail and
parents find themselves totally unable to cope? What are the
root causes of the bewilderment of adults in their relationships
with the young?

Basically, I think that they spring from the pressure and
influences of the world in which the young are growing up and
in which their parents are trying to hold their own. Just as this
book claims no originality and offers no universal solution to the
problems it raises, so it cannot examine in depth the multiplicity
of influences, both for good and evil, to which young people
growing up are particularly vulnerable. Some are political,
some economic, some sociological and spiritual, and already
many books have been written analysing them. Many of these
factors are neither good nor evil in themselves but are capable
of being misused or misunderstood to the great detriment of the
young. Let us look therefore at some of these 'neutral' elements
which nevertheless seem to have the effect of destroying much
of the potential good of young people.

The progresss of scientific knowledge is demonstrably more
rapid today than ever before in the history of the world. The
benefits for mankind from recent discoveries and inventions are
self-evident, but there is the distinct possibility that we may have
created a few monsters which we cannot control because we do
not fully understand them. I am not talking of such cataclysmic
events as the discovery of atomic fission, although it may be
argued that much of the thought of young people nowadays is

37

conditioned by the existence of the Bomb. I am thinking of much more homely and everyday devices, things which on the face of it seem harmless enough but have nevertheless exerted a powerful influence, not always for good—motorbikes, transistor radios, T.V. sets, the contraceptive pill.

The motorbike is obviously a very powerful symbol in teenage culture. Pop-songs, serious novels, films—all these have taken as their inspiration the helmeted, booted, leather-jacketed 'coffee-bar cowboy', doing the ton on our overcrowded roads, his own life and other people's at considerable risk. No doubt the psychologist can analyse much better than I can the sense of power, possibly sexual in origin, which springs from possession of one of these mechanical monsters and the ritual gear which goes with it. There can be no doubt that such unpleasant phenomena as the invasion of seaside resorts by opposing gangs of destructive teenagers have been greatly exacerbated by the fact of the existence of the motorbike. The excitement of the sudden strike and the quick getaway, the exhilaration of speed and the thrill of dicing with death, all to the accompaniment of the admiring cries of one's girl-friend, seem to fill a basic need in some young men. It is thanks to the motorcycle, too, that the teenage gangs are so much more mobile and ubiquitous.

Not only does the transistor radio ensure instant communication within the teenage sub-culture, with the great high priests of pop, the disc-jockeys of Radio One and the pirate radios spreading the gospel for almost twenty-four hours a day, but it also provides the young with a refuge, a world from which all adults may be excluded, by the simple expedient of plugging in a stereophonic earphone. (The fact that the British Medical Journal has declared that this growing practice can do direct damage to the inner ear, leading to permanent deafness, makes little impact either on the young themselves, walking about like zombies in their own little world of perpetual noise, or on the manufacturers of these all but lethal contrivances!) I do not know whether anyone has yet investigated the effect of almost constant noise on the sensibilities and thought-processes of the young, but it might be an interesting study. Large numbers of schoolchildren and students tell us that they cannot do their work except to an accompaniment of pop music. They are not even consciously listening to it, yet if it is absent they feel deprived and unable to concentrate.

I well remember being taken on a conducted tour of a sixth-form college by one of its senior girls. We finished up in the common room, where numbers of students were sitting drinking coffee. Many were talking, some were reading or playing cards, but all against a background of what to my ears was an excruciating din of pop music. It was not the actual music that was at fault but the sheer volume of sound which battered and bludgeoned the mind to a pulp. After trying for five minutes to talk against this, I had to ask my young companion if we could move to another room as I simply could not think straight. Her response was courteous in the extreme, but it was obvious that she had not even been conscious of any noise going on, much less of its being a possible deterrent to civilized conversation.

Television is such a dominant factor in the culture of the Seventies that it needs a whole chapter to itself, and I shall indeed be considering the responsibility of the mass media later on. In the present context, it is perhaps sufficient to indicate the enormous influence which anything as universal, as authoritative and as 'instant' as T.V. can have on the impressionable young. I have already mentioned my doubts about *Top of the Pops* as desirable entertainment, but maybe I am just naturally suspicious of any programme wielding such gigantic power over the young.

I know that many of the older generation are bewildered and saddened by what strikes them as a deliberate cult of ugliness by young people, in clothes, speech, hair-styles, art, music and even facial characteristics. As one writer said to me, 'What a deplorable set of images they will pass on to the subsequent generation!' Without going as far as that in my thinking, I believe there is some truth in the criticism that T.V. perpetually keeps an image of ugliness before its young viewers. I hold no brief for my generation with their photographs of handsome heroes (although I cannot recall that there was anything of the matinee idol about my pin-ups—Clark Gable, Gary Cooper, James Cagney!), but I freely confess that I do not understand why a pretty girl of fifteen or sixteen wants to have a life-size photograph of Jimi Hendrix on her bedroom wall!

But it is the immediacy of T.V. which constitutes its greatest danger. How wonderful it is that we can actually watch man's first steps on the moon as they happen! It is perhaps less wonderful that, if a student in Tokyo throws a petrol-bomb today, it is seen by students all over the world tomorrow. Everyone who watches T.V. must have been struck by the similarity of all demos and protests, whatever the subject and wherever the locale. There can be little doubt that television is the most powerful disseminator of ideas and creator of fashions that the teenage world knows.

Once an idea or a fashion fad has caught the imagination of the young, another feature of our civilization takes over: mass production. Within a matter of days, the discs are in the music shops, the groovy clothes on the racks in Carnaby Street, the paperbacks on the railway bookstalls. A good example of this is the almost suspect haste with which Penguin Books got out *Warwick University Ltd*, the critique of the university's power structure published only two days after the official report by Lord Radcliffe had exonerated Warwick from the charges levelled against it by its rebellious students. Whether E. P. Thompson's account of the relations between industry and the University of Warwick is the balanced and rational account which the *Times Educational Supplement* calls it or a mere polemical tract designed to pour oil on burning embers is beside the point. It is the publishers' essay in instant history which is interesting.

The proliferation of paperback literature is yet another of the factors in modern life which are of the greatest importance. I have heard it said that the 'rot set in' with the freeing of *Lady Chatterley's Lover* from censorship. Now this is a very debatable point which I do not propose to go into at this juncture, but one thing is certain: court case or no court case, *Lady C.* would have made little impact on the reading public in general and the young in particular had it not been readily available in paperback at the cost of only a few shillings.

I can still remember the excitement of the first Penguin

editions; of being able, as a penniless student, to buy good books cheaply. As I see young people thronging the bookstalls, I am delighted by the tremendous choice of reading matter now available to them at reasonable prices, even though no longer at the sixpence which we paid for Penguins. Yet as one looks more closely at some of the books, one begins to wonder whether it might not have been better for our children if they had remained in the relative inaccessibility of hard covers; even if one is, as I am, basically opposed to censorship.

It is perhaps in the field of sexual freedom and responsibility that we see most clearly the paramount importance of modern scientific invention. The contraceptive pill has given young women, both married and unmarried, complete control over their sexual lives. There is not the smallest reason why fear of pregnancy need deter a girl from sleeping with her boy-friend. Even if she cannot get 'on the Pill', as the inelegant phrase goes, knowledge of other contraceptive methods is so widespread and so freely available that young people in their teens and twenties would have to be very dim indeed not to be able to get all the information they needed. Now of course, should the worst come to the worst, there is always abortion or, if that cannot be procured, an adoption society will take care of the unfortunate little accident. Even venereal disease has lost many of its terrors in this age of antibiotics, and one hears of quite young boys and girls who have had repeatedly to visit clinics because they have become infected over and over again and think nothing of it. It is not so long ago that I was watching a programme on T.V. where a doctor looked forward to the time when all young people would be inoculated against syphilis just as nowadays they are against polio and smallpox.

These are only a few of the forces at work in the world today which are having the greatest possible influence on the lives of our children. Everything that I have mentioned can be and often is a powerful influence for good. After all, who can deny that the possibility of controlling the over-population of the world is a good thing, that cheap books, television and radio are wonderful tools in the hands of the educators? But far too often the influence is a malign one.

A less obvious consequence of the rapid and intensive progress of scientific knowledge has been the weakening of the once powerful sanction of religious authority. Ever since Darwin's *Origin of Species* cast doubts on the historical accuracy of the Old Testament, increasing numbers of thinking people have been rejecting religion as the unquestionable basis for moral behaviour. One might say that this is not new, that we have always had atheists, agnostics and scientific humanists with us. What *is* new is their proselytizing zeal, and, for the first time, they have the mass-media at their disposal for the dissemination of their views. Scientific knowledge is no longer the preserve of the educated few: every schoolchild knows enough to question the truths of religion and to follow the arguments of its opponents, who seem just as keen to convert Christians to their way of thinking as any Jesuit missionary was to convert pagans to Christianity.

There is a hymn which begins 'My God, I love Thee, not because I hope for Heaven thereby'. It may be true that in an age of faith people loved God for worthier reasons than a selfish desire for pie in the sky, but I feel pretty sure that large numbers of both young and old *feared* Him because of what might happen to them if they did not. In other words, the thought of the everlasting bonfire kept a lot of people on the straight and narrow path. Now, I am perfectly ready to admit that it is unworthy to do right for the wrong reasons, but it did make life much easier for the young! And infinitely easier for their parents and teachers. There was only one reason why you should not lie, steal, fornicate, dishonour your parents and the Sabbath day, covet, or break any of the other commandments, and that was because to do so was *wrong*. Just as to be truthful, honest, chaste, filial, pious was *right*. Why was it wrong or right? Because God said so in the Bible. And if you did wrong, you jolly well went to hell and serve you right too. Even if doing what was right did not seem to bring you very much in the way of this world's goods, whereas the wicked flourished like the green bay tree, you had the infinite satisfaction of knowing that you would get your reward in heaven. The story of Dives and Lazarus must have been a great comfort to the deserving poor.

All that certainty has been swept away with the flood of scientific discoveries, from evolution to the Dead Sea Scrolls, a diet of which, gulped down and imperfectly digested, has only succeeded in giving us all moral indigestion. This whole question of the decline of moral standards is so fundamental to our problem that I shall return to examine it in much greater detail in a later chapter. At the moment, let us be content with a sidelong glance at it as a consequence of the spread of scientific knowledge, with its consequent slackening of the grip of religion.

One of the catch-phrases of the age is 'the Affluent Society'; and although many of my correspondents living on small fixed incomes would smile sadly at any such phrase, it is true that the vast majority of the population of Britain is better off than ever before. Despite penal taxation, high prices and ever-increasing wage demands, very few people actually deny themselves the things they want. In fact, most of those who complain about their low wages do not go short of necessities but are crying out for a bigger share of luxuries.

Recently the B.B.C. was interviewing strikers at a north-country factory. After complaining bitterly that they were not getting a living wage, their spokesman solemnly warned that if the strike dragged on for much longer many of the men would have to sell their cars! All the things which were unheard of in working-class homes and indeed in many middle-class homes before the war are common-place now: telephone, car, washing-machine, refrigerator, T.V., hi-fi equipment, tape-recorder, cine-camera, dish-washer, deep-freeze—many if not all of these are now taken for granted in large numbers of households. Hire-purchase has brought what used to be thought of as unattainable luxuries within the grasp of most people, just as package tours have taken thousands abroad who before the war would not have ventured beyond Blackpool or Southend.

Now, this is an excellent thing in itself and no one could possibly cavil at a rising standard of living, with more and more of the people who work to produce consumer goods actually doing some of the consuming themselves. However, one is bound to recognize the fact that acquisitiveness and exhibitionism are not perhaps the most attractive of all human instincts, and built-in obsolescence and powerful advertising media are creating a society where possession of more and more material things, each one bigger and better than the Joneses', seems to be the only goal, and in which not to have what others have seems deprivation. My generation, brought up in the hungry Thirties, was taught that to say 'I want' was rude and greedy. 'I should like' was just permissible; but we well knew that more often than not we could not have what we desired for the money was not forthcoming. Since none of our friends possessed the things which we coveted, we did not feel seriously deprived and wasted little time crying for the moon.

Children nowadays find themselves in a very different society. Everywhere the accent is on possessions, and it is perfectly true that the more one has the more one wants. Parents who, when young, probably got an orange, some crackers and a few nuts at Christmas, with one or two small toys if they were lucky, think nothing of spending thirty pounds on one toy motor car or a tape-recorder for their child. From the time a baby is able to crawl, expensive clothes and toys are showered upon him and in far too many homes 'I want' is followed by immediate acquisition, or, if it is not, then there are tears and tantrums. Small wonder that so many grow to maturity hardly ever having heard the word 'no', and take as their motto: 'I want what I want when I want it for the world owes me *luxury* living.' Students complain that their grants are insufficient for them to buy books, and some of them make this an excuse to steal books from libraries and shops, blandly stating that they do not see why they should go without when the shops have plenty. Yet these same students see nothing contradictory in running a car, smoking twenty cigarettes a day and doing their share of drinking, as well as spending most of their vacations travelling abroad.

Many young people, especially those working and still living at home, seem to have little or no sense of the value of money. They continue to be waited on hand and foot by their mothers and sometimes pay nothing at all for their keep. Others pay a derisory amount which no landlady would accept for similar services. This leaves them with no responsibilities and a pocketful of money, easy prey for commercial exploitation and the cult of materialism. Round about Christmas-time 1969, I listened to a B.B.C. reporter asking girls in their teens and early twenties what they would spend on a present for the boy-friend. I do not think that these girls were boasting or lying, and most of them mentioned sums between twenty and forty pounds. Surely I am not alone in finding this profoundly shocking when one considers that an old-age pensioner has five pounds a week on which to live?

Of all the age-groups, it is the affluent young who are most open to exploitation, the first generation of mugs with money and fair game for the spoilers. With no responsibilities and accountable to no one, urged by their pop idols to live for today for tomorrow they will be too old, they pour out their money in an unending flood on ephemeral and trumpery rubbish which the advertisers persuade them that they must have to be 'with it'.

For years now, women of my age have despaired of fashion and ceased to buy the fashion magazines, for everything has been geared to the under-twenties, the dolly-girls who will buy a dress one week and throw it away the next when a new fad is promoted by the admen. The absolutely universal cult of the mini-skirt completely ignored the older woman, so that the over-thirties had to look either dowdy by not wearing it or ridiculous by wearing it, just as the current cult of the trouser-suit conveniently disregards the fact that few women over twenty are built for trousers.

So much in present-day fashions seems to be exaggerated, extreme, garish and sensational, made to appeal exclusively to the young and silly. I almost cancelled the order for my favourite Sunday paper after reading on the Woman's Page an excessively idiotic eulogy of 'fun furs'—rabbit dyed purple, so much more to be desired than 'dowdy old mink'. Now, there is absolutely no reason why young readers of that newspaper should not spend their money on purple rabbit if they feel so inclined; but there is equally no reason why Mum, who probably pays for the paper anyway, should be made to feel a fool and a has-been because she would prefer mink, and after saving for twenty years has just managed to get a stole. Like so much of the propaganda beamed at the teenager, this kind of article deliberately tries to emphasize the generation gap and to build up in the young a sense of their own infinite superiority to their elders, whose values they are subtly being taught to discard and despise.

For this is the most deplorable result of creating a teenage cult purely in order to exploit it commercially. As soon as a group becomes separate from the rest of society, with specialized tastes and needs and different values, then it develops a dangerous sense of superiority and makes a virtue of its differences, even of its weaknesses. Flattered and courted on all sides by commercial interests and the admen, indulged by parents, deferred to by vote-catching politicians, their ego inflated by the hot air of the mass media, the immature can hardly be blamed for assuming that they are simply the most important group in society and, indeed, the only group with any right to be heard. They believe their power to be unlimited, that 'all you need is love'—or at any rate youth—and then everything can be effortlessly achieved. The fantastic commercial success of untalented amateurs in the pop world—uncouth, amoral, barely literate, incoherent in thought and speech—on nothing more than the dubious ability to bawl into a microphone and hold down three basic chords on a guitar (I am not referring to the Beatles, who are or at least were in a class by themselves, but to some others whom clever promoters have boosted to stardom) leads their childish worshippers to discount education and hard work as necessary for success, since success in this affluent society has come to mean only one thing: money.

Unfortunately for these young emperors, strutting before the world in their invisible new clothes, however much flatterers and parasites may try to keep up their delusions of grandeur, the real forces in modern society remain singularly unimpressed by them. As soon as they come up against adult authority and find themselves in adult situations, they are exposed in all their nakedness and soon discover that they have absolutely no power at all, even over their own lives, much less over the lives of their much-despised elders.

And, of course, this is when the crunch comes: you cannot bring up a child from the cradle to believe himself omnipotent, the centre of the universe, suddenly reveal to him that he is really quite unimportant and virtually powerless in an adult world and expect him not to lash out at you in impotent fury. Accustomed to having everything he wants as soon as he wants it, accountable to no one, never having to make a decision of more importance than the colour of his shirt, suddenly he feels the cold winds of reality blowing about him. As he approaches adulthood he begins to perceive, albeit dimly, that the world is not his oyster and that no one seems to think that he is owed a living. And that is when the trouble starts.

It is easy to see why commercial exploiters foster the teenage group feeling, which is, in any case, typical of childhood and adolescence. The young have always tended to herd together in gangs, 'secret' societies from which grown-ups were rigidly excluded. But there is another factor which encourages young people to take refuge in this tribal society of theirs, and that is the increasing depersonalization of all other groupings. At an age when one's own identity is the most important thing in the world, it is very easy to feel completely lost in a society composed of mammoth trade unions, huge conurbations, gigantic monopoly industries and, as the comprehensive principle takes root, larger and larger schools. I must admit that one of the things which worries me about comprehensive schools is their sheer size. Many of them have been built and more are planned for over two thousand pupils, and no matter what financial or administrative or even educational (viable size of sixth form?) reasons there may be for these monsters, I cannot believe that they will not have an adverse effect on the development of personality and identity. A world consisting of huge groupings tends to be a frightening world, and one sees why the young feel that they have to seek protection from it in the safety of their own sub-cult.

The pity of it is that so many of these influences which are working against young people are also full of potential good. Traditional religion may have been weakened by the growth of scientific knowledge and the spread of anti-religious propaganda by humanists and secularists, but the way has surely been opened to a clearer appreciation of truth and of the need for

47

moral responsibility. It is obviously easier, especially for parents, if children simply do 'right' for fear of hell or hope of heaven. It is surely much better that they should be helped to look at the great question of right and wrong and still make what the traditionalists would call the 'right' decision. Now that greater affluence has largely removed poverty and unemployment, there is less desperate incentive to hard work and self-control, but at the same time millions have been given immeasurable opportunities for a much freer choice of work and more satisfaction in it. Though young people may feel adrift and anonymous in great cities, it is here that they find all kinds of cultural influences readily accessible and that the horizons of the mind may be widened.

I do not think that one can pose the question of whether society today is better or worse for young people growing up, although my correspondents clearly think that it is worse, since so many of them express pity for children living in such a difficult world. We simply do not know the answer, but I am inclined to think that for a great many young people, perhaps for the majority, society is greatly better than in previous ages. I hope though that I have at least demonstrated that it is *different* from the society in which most of their parents and teachers grew up, and that anyone who cares about the young and wants to be of use to them must take into account these differences.

One thing is certain: even though we may not be qualified to decide once and for all whether the world of today is better or worse than that of yesterday, at least we are probably in a slightly better position to form a balanced judgement than are the young. After all, we were alive yesterday, and although our views may be nostalgic and seen through rose-coloured spectacles we can at least look at the two worlds with some factual knowledge of them both.

I confess (and the young must forgive me for this!) to feeling gentle amusement on being told by a young man from Brentwood that 'intolerance is the hallmark of your generation, and it may stem from its adulation of Fascism in the Thirties. The conduct and achievement of your generation has been on the whole a disgrace to the tradition of which I am proud to be an heir.' Now, this young heir of the heroic tradition (he goes on to speak of Churchill, whom he seems to admire) has my full permission to call me intolerant if he so wishes, but I am damned if he is going to get away with calling me, or my generation, Fascist. What, I wonder, does he think we were doing—some of *my* friends at any rate—in Spain and Abyssinia in the Thirties, not to mention that little conflict which began, if my ageing memory serves me, in 1939? But then he would hardly know, for he was not born then. Nor would have been later if my generation had been as adulatory of Fascism as he thinks!

The same young man goes on to accuse me of 'Victorian magisterialism', regardless of the fact that the good Queen's *grandson* had been on the throne some considerable time before ever I was born.

Too many of the critical young prate intolerantly of my generation as though we had been born in the Dark Ages, and do not hesitate to tell us about what things were really like in our day . . . years before they were born. Only a few months ago, some friends and I were almost reduced to apoplexy by being told all about Dunkirk and the Battle of Britain by a girl in her twenties. She was quite fantastically misinformed, having obviously been subjected to some rather pernicious propaganda. She told us, to our astonishment, that in 1940 the British were all told that Dunkirk was a victory whereas it was really a defeat; that German bombing all but broke us and the people of London and the big cities were ready to sue for peace, only being controlled by vicious martial law; that the R.A.F. was thoroughly demoralized towards the end of the Battle of Britain and on the verge of surrender. Although singly and collectively we told her that all this was a load of rubbish, that we had been at Dunkirk, fought in Spitfires, endured the bombing of London, she insisted that she was right and we were wrong. It was useless for us to protest that she had not been born until after the war had ended: she knew better than we did how blind and craven and misled we had all been in the bad old days.

I know that there is nothing more infuriating for the young than to be told that because we are older we must of necessity be

49

wiser. This is certainly not true, but we are at least more experienced in the ways of the world and we do know how it was when we were younger, even though, as I say, distance may have lent enchantment to the view.

This is why we must not abdicate from judgement, why we must be prepared to look critically though fairly at the modern world, be aware of its dangers and difficulties at the same time as we appreciate its advantages, and help those who have missed the stepping-stones and are floundering in the morass to find firm ground again. For, after all, we have made the same journey in our time. Some of the stepping-stones may now be unsafe or submerged, someone may have torn down the signposts, the pitfalls may now be in different places, but it's the same old swamp that we had to wade through, the mud is still as sticky and the green patches as tempting and treacherous as ever they were. It is useless to shout to the young travellers to go back for this they cannot do; it is stupid to give them false confidence by telling them that they are so much better navigators than we were and cannot possibly lose the way. But it is criminal irresponsibility to turn our backs on them and let them sink or swim.

4

The Abdicating Adult

This chapter is starting from the premise that young people need and have a right to expect help in the process of growing up. This is probably the greatest responsibility which adults have to accept, and many of them find it difficult. It is all the more so because very few children will not, at some stage in their development, reject such help with varying degrees of impatience and violence. No generation in history succeeding another has not differed from its predecessors; it is a fact of psychological life not only that such disagreements occur almost automatically but that it is vital that they do so, for without them social reform and progress would be severely hampered if not stalled altogether. Only by *healthy* antagonism between the generations can the inevitable compromise and progress be attained.

Yet I am sure that the Cambridge undergraduate goes too far when he writes to me: 'It is the very concept of loving guidance that young people are rebelling against. We have to escape from the suffocating bosom of the elder generation—hairstyles and music are merely symbols of our discontent and antipathy to repression and reactionary discipline.' For the whole point is that discipline rooted and grounded in love—and I make no apology for coming back to that concept again and again—is neither repressive nor reactionary and certainly not stifling. Young people today are apparently so self-assured, but they are almost tragic in their vulnerability, exposed as they are to the twin onslaughts of materialism and commercial exploitation. What they need is to be in touch with an imperturbable adult who is not easily pushed off balance or emotionally disturbed, against whom in the anxious years their storms can break and break again. They do not want to be given the intolerable responsibility of making their own decisions before they have the mental and emotional maturity to do so. Every child should be given responsibility as young as possible, but it must be measured to his capacity, enough to stretch him but not too much, so as to become burdensome or oppressive. Even at considerable cost to his parents and teachers—cost of time and temper!—he must never be left completely alone to make decisions which will be positively harmful to him. For once an adult adopts the policy of 'anything for a quiet life', and so gives the child all he wants, where does it stop?

One thing we may be certain of, the child's demands will become more and more outrageous for the very reason that he is daring you to say 'no' to him. Neither is there very much future in expecting logic or sweet reason from an adolescent. Your teenage daughter is quite likely to upbraid you bitterly for insisting that she be in at what you call a reasonable hour, but she is equally likely to burst into floods of tears and say that you don't care what happens to her if you allow her to stop out all night.

Which brings us back inevitably to the phrase *rooted and grounded in love*. Children must know that we care about them and that it is because we care that we are not going to allow them to run into danger. I have known young people for many years and could quote so many examples: the boy who said that to live without rules would be like living in a quicksand; the weeping girl who, when her mother asked her what she wanted to do, wailed in despair, 'I don't want you to ask me, I want you to tell me'; the senior girl from a school where, because of a change of Head, discipline had become very slack, who said to me, 'It's horrible. We feel as if nobody cares what we do.'

I have already made the point that we do the young a grave disservice when we abdicate from judgement. For their sake, let adults realize that adolescence is a most unstable age, both physically and emotionally, and that the bewilderment of the young is an appeal to us for values. The teenager is bombarded on all sides with pernicious propaganda which assures him that all his age-group like this and dislike that, admire these pop stars and have tired of others, wear certain clothes and do their hair a certain way; and that if he is different, if he is not with it, then he is somehow abnormal. This slavish adherence to group opinion is a most serious threat to the development of personality, and adults must help the young to resist these pressures. This seems to me so simple and obvious that I am in despair when I see so many adults unable or unwilling to undertake the responsibility. What are the reasons for this failure of adult responsibility with its catastrophic results for the young?

Let me begin by quoting a letter sent to a Canadian newspaper by a schoolgirl called Sally. She writes:

> When you come right down to it, it's the parents who are paying for the students' education and ask any parent if he wants his child disciplined at school and he will undoubtedly answer in the affirmative. How can a mother convince her daughter it's not old-fashioned to be neat, clean and feminine when she's allowed to do and wear what she wants to at school? How can a student who has had no discipline at school find it not difficult to follow the necessary maxims of society? I feel that students today are being handed everything they want on a silver platter and that it's not only dangerous but lethal. In a world populated by over three billion people it's imperative we learn there are some things we can't have, some people we have to put up with and some rules we have to follow. What better place to learn them than at school?

This goes right to the heart of the matter in stating that responsibility for the young belongs to all adults and that if any abdicate, the task of the others is that much harder. Parents, alas, are often the worst offenders. Was it Bernard Shaw who said that the last people who ought to have children are parents? Far too often one hears it said of a tiresome four-year-old, 'He'll soon be going to school and the teacher will sort him out.' Mother has failed to sort out her one child but confidently expects a teacher to cope with forty.

Recently, the father of a boy convicted of possessing drugs attacked the school and the education authority for not taking steps to inform and advise parents about the drug problem, despite the fact that the pupils had been given talks by teachers and the police. What sort of sheltered life had that father lived if he did not already know that there was a drug problem among young people without having specifically to be told so by his son's teachers? He complained that the dangers of drugs had not been 'spelt out' to his son by the school. Was it not therefore incumbent upon *him* to do some spelling-out himself?

This whole business of parents leaving it to the schools under- lines the vital point that guidance of the teenager, if it is to be effective, must begin long before the teens are reached—in the cradle, in fact. The selfishness, the callousness, the greed, the self-indulgence which sometimes seem to seize upon teenagers with such dire results do not begin in the teens. They have usually been building up right through babyhood and child- hood, masked by the easy acquisition of material satisfactions and the evasion of unpleasant issues, until the fierce pressures of the teens from within and without find young people defence- less because they are unpractised in resistance. One hopes that not too many of the parents reading this book will hear their own words in the following quotations, but I feel sure that very many will have heard them on the lips of others.

'We can't understand why she's like that: we've always given her everything she wanted.'

'We only wanted her to be happy.'

'We want him to have what we didn't have.'

'Never mind, she'll grow out of it and you're only young once.'

'Don't ask me, ask your father.'

'Don't ask me, ask your mother.'

When I say that all adults have a duty to help the young, I do not only refer to the obvious groups like parents, teachers, youth leaders, probation officers and the police. This duty belongs to every one of us in every walk of life though some, because their influence is greater, bear a heavier responsibility than others. What of the responsibility of the doctor who overprescribes dangerous drugs, knowing that by so doing he may deliver them into the hands of pushers? What of the factory foreman who ignores or even encourages unpleasant initiation rites such as almost burned an apprentice to death recently, or who discourages a boy from working too hard and teaches him restrictive practices and bad time-keeping? What of the hairdresser, the dress-designer, the store-manager, the politician? And what, oh what, of the T.V. script-writer and producer, the film-director, the novelist, the song-writer? The list is endless, because we all, in one way or another, are in touch with young people and are in a position to influence and guide them.

Why is it then that so many of us, when we are not doing the young positive harm, cravenly refrain from doing them any good?

First, I think that there is among adults a great uncertainty about our own moral standards. The undermining of religious faith has affected us just as much as it has affected our children. We have stopped going to church and certainly we have stopped taking our children. We make the excuse that we can be just as religious without attending church, even that we are a good deal better than plenty of the hypocrites who do go, and without the authority of the Church to back us up we are disinclined to dictate to or exercise authority upon the young. We hear the faith of our own childhood attacked on every side and we no longer know what to teach our children. When we turn to church leaders for guidance, we get *Honest to God*, and either we do not understand a word of it or else we are left with the uneasy feeling that the God we thought the Church believed in no longer exists. Deprived of the old religious certainties of right and wrong, we struggle to make our own guide-lines. If our children are to embark on perilous seas without the old charts, we feel that we must at least teach them how to make new ones. So we try to think seriously about morality, and immediately we discover that there is something called 'the new morality', which seems to prove that there cannot possibly be any absolutes like the concepts of right and wrong. Morality, we learn, and from very authoritative sources, is relative. Who, they ask, has the right to determine what morality is? It is, after all, only a social convention, and today's immorality will be tomorrow's norm. There is no absolute authority and one man's opinion is as good as the next.

When young people complain of the pressure exerted on them by this materialistic get-rich-quick world and the 'difficulties which face the progressively minded young adults in today's capitalist-orientated society', they seem to forget that their elders are often suffering from exactly the same pressures and without youth's resilience in the battle to withstand them. After all, we have been fighting for rather a long time and we are getting tired.

It is unfortunate that so many adults have given up the struggle and that the example which is set the young of greedy, selfish, anti-social and downright dishonest behaviour adds still further to the latter's confusion. One of the less pleasant hangovers from the war is what I would call the 'black-market mentality', the idea that it is perfectly all right to get a bit extra on the side because everyone else is engaged in some kind of fiddle. Income-tax evasion is practically a patriotic duty, if we are to believe some of our friends; smuggling (which has always held a fascination for the English—'Watch the wall, my darling, while the gentlemen go by') has added currency-fiddling to the more usual ploys of seeing how many cigarettes and spirits one can sneak past the Customs officers.

I am not sure whether restricting the amount of foreign currency the man in the street could spend on his holiday to the ridiculous sum of fifty pounds benefited the economy by the large sums of which we were told by the late Chancellor. What I am sure of is that this regulation turned us into a nation of swindlers. How many travellers abroad could truthfully say that they had never spent one penny more than the sum to which they were legally entitled? I have been on holiday amongst a group of otherwise respectable, honest citizens, where one of the main topics of conversation, in front of the children, was how much foreign currency had been fiddled, by one dishonest means after another, from smuggling five-pound notes in the wife's bra to getting a friendly doctor to certify that one was ill enough to require an extra seven pounds a day. One man told me that his boss, on learning that he was going abroad on holiday, offered to arrange a deposit of a thousand pounds in a foreign bank! When, in all innocence, I asked a couple who seemed to have been abroad for months how they managed on the fifty-pound allowance, they laughed and said, '*Is* there a fifty-pound allowance?'

What is the use of preaching to the young about the virtues of honest labour in a country with our shocking record of strikes, wildcat and otherwise? Of the evils of self-indulgence when industry takes almost two weeks' holiday at Christmas in order to recover from its hangover? Of the dangers of addictive drugs when deaths from alcoholism and lung cancer continue to rise at an appalling rate? Not only are we so unsure of ourselves on moral grounds that we virtually contract out of the responsibility for guiding others, but also many of us transgress the very code that we teach, and work on the cynical principle of 'Do as I say, not as I do'.

Just as the spread of what I might call 'instant humanism' has undermined adult belief in religion as a moral sanction, so pop psychology, with much of its emphasis on the inhibitive and destructive factors in old-fashioned discipline, has contributed further to adult uncertainty. Very few of those who quote psychology have actually made a serious study of the subject, but there is a widely held belief, especially among parents, that children—and particularly young children—should not be thwarted in any way.

The famous Dr Spock has recently protested against his title of 'father of the modern permissiveness'. He believes, as I do, that 'the modern crop of youths is not only reassuring, they are inspiring. Our only hope is their thoughtfulness, their idealism, and realism.' At the same time he has gone on record as deploring the behaviour of young Americans who have fled abroad rather than face conscription, and reliance on drugs appals him. In the revised edition of his famous book *Baby and Child Care* he comes down quite definitely on the side of chastity: 'Going steady cheapens love' and 'The wish to preserve sexual intimacy is not just puritanism'. His own sons apparently remember him as quite authoritarian and not hesitating to spank them when the occasion demanded it. In fact, we are told that he is convinced that the linking of his name with permissiveness is the result of his books being published at the same time as a report which tried to prove that a baby should be fed on demand and not to a prearranged timetable. Spock had been impressed with Freud's theory about sexual repression in infancy and believed,

I am sure rightly, that inflexibility in any form was no way to bring up a child. He maintains that his ideas and those of the report became confused in the mind of the public. 'Parents thought that if you could let a baby decide how to eat, then you could let him decide how to sleep, how to play and so on. I was alarmed. There should be firm leadership from a parent to make a child happier.'

Yet the fact remains that half-baked and half-digested ideas about the absolute necessity of leaving a child 'free' and 'happy' have produced what has come to be known as the 'Spock-marked child', whether or not that name is unfair to Dr Spock. To be 'progressive' has become the 'in' thing, and the opposite of progressive is apparently 'reactionary'. There seems to be no middle way. I have never struck a child in my life, having never seen the necessity, but I would not under any circumstances label a parent or teacher who used corporal punishment judiciously a 'sadistic monster', as seems to be fashionable nowadays.

It makes me very angry to hear critics of those teachers who plead for the retention of their ultimate deterrent, sneering that any adult who cannot control a child without hitting it is unfit to teach. I should rather enjoy locking up one of these experts in a classroom full of problem children and seeing how long it would be before he was either screaming to be let out or else had murdered a few of them. Teachers are assaulted, stabbed, spat upon, sworn at, subjected to every kind of obscene insult and humiliation by their pupils—what is one to think of the pretty young teacher who was waylaid by boys and had her knickers torn off?—and yet they are to have no effective weapon against hooligans. To listen to the 'progressives' one would think that every desperate teacher who uses the cane as a last resort is Gilles de Rais dripping with the blood of innocent child victims. How far from the truth can you get?

There is much in 'progressive' education which causes me some unease. With really good teachers and a leavening of hard learning, nothing but good can come of modern developments in the primary school; but there is a distinct danger where teachers are unsure of how to adapt the new ideas or where

misunderstanding of their real aims causes them to throw overboard any semblance of order or any attempt at formal 'work'.
In the last ten years or so, I and many secondary teachers have
noticed a definite change in the eleven-year-olds coming up
from the primary school.

I shall almost certainly be attacked by the progressives for
saying this, and no doubt they will produce facts and figures to
prove me wrong, so I shall only say that it has been *my impression*
and that of many of my colleagues that these children are much
less literate and numerate than ever before. Each year we have
had to spend more time teaching the basic skills and drills that,
formerly, children knew long before they left the junior school.
Writing, spelling, punctuation all *seem* (I shall put it no more
strongly than that) to have deteriorated; and as for grammar,
this has become an unknown subject, as teachers of language
know to their cost. It is all very well concentrating on the audio-
visual approach to the teaching of French, but I still maintain
that there is some place left for the mastery of grammar unless
we are to give up any idea of producing even the occasional
scholar in the old-fashioned sense of the word—and how do you
teach French or Latin grammar to a class which does not even
know what is meant by number and gender and to whom you
have to teach the words *masculine* and *feminine*? I remember
exclaiming bitterly to a colleague that I had to give some sex
instruction to my class before embarking on the difference
between *le* and *la*!

Children taught in progressive schools are, we are told, much
more lively-minded, have more intellectual curiosity, than those
taught by traditional methods. I do not entirely go along with
this from my own experience, although it may be so and I shall
not argue about it. I have found them more restless, unable to
sit down for more than a few minutes at a time because they
have been used to wandering about their open-plan schools at
will; less able to concentrate, especially on tasks presenting
some difficulty, because they have not been encouraged to do
things which they did not want to do, nor to persevere when the
novelty wore off and things became a little boring.

I have never found children of that age afraid of me or of any kind of authority, but, latterly, their self-confidence has occasionally shown itself in a rather disconcerting fashion. A friendly child is a delightful thing, an impudent one is not, and I have seen eighteen-year-old sixth formers and junior members of staff considerably taken aback by the unruly behaviour of children on their first day in secondary school. Nobody wants to go back to the bad old days when children were seen and not heard, but it is a pity if no one else can be heard for the din they are making.

Some friends of mind recently visited a well-known progressive school with a view to sending their son to it. Arriving for their appointment with the Headmaster, they rang his door-bell. The door opened and they were confronted with a totally naked child of about ten who greeted them with the words, 'What the bloody hell do you want?' They did not wait for the interview but turned about and went home.

Like so much to which the young are exposed, new ideas such as the 'play way' and 'discovery learning' are excellent in themselves but can easily be misunderstood and misapplied, to the great detriment of the children. Much emphasis is placed by the progressives on the idea that education is a preparation for life, and therefore it should not concern itself with dry-as-dust factual information but should deal with the whole child. Now, leaving aside the plain fact that many children actually enjoy acquiring what some of their educators contemptuously dismiss as 'dry-as-dust' (I remember the highly intelligent girl whose school taught French with the very latest language-laboratory methods and Latin with the same old grammar grind of bygone days saying to me plaintively that she *wished* they learned French the way they learned Latin!), is it really a preparation for life only to do delightful, interesting, easy things and for only as long as you feel like it? Sally from Canada asked whether there was a better place than school to learn that 'there are some things we can't have, some people we have to put up with and some rules we have to follow'. I would add that there is some work that we have to do, however dull, difficult or even downright unpleasant it may sometimes be, and that the sooner we learn that life is not all 'play way', the better for us.

I have no intention here of going into the question of selection, except to say that whereas one's school may no longer select, life unfortunately does. The current outcry is against examinations, either to abolish them altogether or else to make them so that no one can fail, which is the same thing, since a test which no one can fail is not a test. In every way nowadays it seems the 'in' thing to decry excellence, to reduce everything and everyone to a uniform mediocrity lest the less favoured should feel deprived. I can see no point whatsoever in bringing up children to imagine that life is fair—if ever a child complains to me, 'It isn't fair!' I am tempted to reply, 'Probably not, but that's life.' If throughout their childhood and schooldays they are protected from anything dull, difficult, a bit boring, unfair, anything in which other people seem to have an advantage, children are going to get a very nasty shock when faced with the real life for which these pleasant schooldays are supposed to be preparing them. Let no one write to accuse me of deliberately wanting to make children's lives a misery. But if all work and no play makes Jack a dull boy, there are some grounds for thinking that all play and no work will make him a delinquent one.

Parents, who are quite as deeply concerned as in the past with the welfare of their children, retire bewildered, their confidence as to how best to guide them completely shattered, when the experts tell them that all the ways in which they were brought up are not only wrong but dangerous and even positively antisocial. Mother must not teach a small child, obviously longing to learn, how to read; Father, even with an Honours degree, must not teach Johnny maths, however desperate his clever child may be to get to grips with numbers. Education has become so much cluttered up with gimmicks and expensive hardware that the amateurs—the parents—are afraid to interfere and the professionals have it all their own way. Only nowadays the professionals are not always the teachers, for they are too often at the mercy of each and every crank in Education (with a capital E) who, never having to set foot in a classroom, has nothing better to do than to dream up new theories.

I shall never forget being told, when I asked a university

lecturer in Education whether there might not be some slowing-down of the educational process for clever children in small comprehensive schools, 'It will not matter if a clever boy cannot take "O" levels before he is seventeen, he will have the satisfaction of knowing that he has helped his weaker brethren along the road of life.' There are far too many woolly-minded sentimentalists behind some of our current educational theories, creating a ramshackle school system which denigrates authority, decries hard work and intellectual excellence and, by blinding them with science, denies the interested parents the opportunity to help with their children's education as well as the right to decide how or where they shall be educated.

So the relationship of adult society with the young has come to be strongly marked by a permissive, sometimes even an apologetic, attitude. With no support from religion, criticized by the psychologist and excluded by the educationalist, it is no wonder parents simply contract out of guiding the young.

This insistence by the experts that they and they alone know the answers tends to give parents an inferiority complex in their dealings with their children. This is exacerbated by the fact that, in a large number of homes, the children are—or at least seem to be—better educated than their parents. In the things which matter, I do not believe that they always are, but most of them do manage to know a little about a lot of things which did not come into their parents' schooling at all, and it becomes very easy for the arrogant young to tell their parents in superior tones that they do not know what they are talking about. This is sometimes sufficiently true for it to be difficult for the parents to answer back. Nothing is more calculated to make parents feel that they have no right to lay down the law about anything than a feeling of educational inferiority, and the young are quick enough to exploit it.

Yet one more weakening of the parental grip is a side-effect of the Welfare State. No one at all could possibly deplore the removal of stark economic pressures by State-administered social security; but do not some of us tend to lean more and more on the State, or at any rate on some mysterious body whom we refer to as *they*, not only in the matter of our civic responsibilities but even in parental and filial obligations? There is rarely any question now of young people waiting until they feel that they can afford to get married or to have children. It is assumed that they have the *right* to a wife and children, even at the same time as they are enjoying (if that is the right word) a university education, and that it is the duty of the State, of *them*, to pay for all these things. The fact that *they* are not some magic money-making machine but the wretched tax-payers of their country does not always seem to be realized by the demanding young. I admit that I got just a little bit tired of being told by young critics of students' *right* to be at university. No one seemed inclined to talk of *responsibility* in this context.

Once parents begin to think that other people should do their job for them, either because they have been brainwashed into believing that the experts can do it better or because they think they have a right to have the job done for them, the family as an influence for good in society is finished, and it follows from this that, if parents abdicate from real parenthood, the children will feel no filial ties and will have no compunction about bundling the old folks off into a home as soon as they decently can.

Some people would argue that the family has already ceased to exist—certainly what I might call the *extended* family, with grandparents still in a position of authority and lots of uncles and aunts about the house, is no longer a reality. In a household where there may be an abdicating father, wholly given over to the pursuit of his career (often with good intentions because he wants to be a 'good provider'), where mother, if she is not also working, is absorbed in her bridge club, her committees, her social work, and where there may be no other near adult relatives, a boy may grow to young manhood without ever making a close and meaningful relationship with an adult. Is it to be wondered at that such a boy will develop an aggressive suspicion of all adult authority, seeking refuge from his loneliness in his own age-group and trying desperately to win their approval by continual and spectacular defiance of the adult world?

The changing position of women in the world obviously contributed to the loosening of family ties. I cannot see how the family can avoid becoming a less tightly knit unit when both parents work outside the home. I am not saying that married women should not work: this would be absurd, especially since I know that, had I married, I should have expected to go on with my job; but it should be recognized that there is likely to be a problem of the age-groups growing away from each other and having less and less time for each other or interest in each other. Slowly but surely, a situation may develop in which hurt and puzzled people find themselves shouting at one another across the generation gap and do not know why each cannot understand what the other is saying.

5

The 'Effluent' Society

The reasons why so many older people have adopted such a spineless and compromising attitude to the young are so fundamental to our problem that we must continue to look for them. We have already seen something of the effect of the decline of religion (what Richard Hoggart called 'the death of the Protestant ethic'), the spread of pop psychology, the Welfare State mentality and the break-up of the family. We have admitted adult failure in the field of personal example, the entry of the teenager into the adult world being too often an entry into a world of coarser standards. Are there other reasons? I think there are.

This may seem extremely far fetched, but perhaps it is worth considering. In the First World War millions of young men were slaughtered like cattle for no very good reason. The massacre was not on the same scale in the Second World War but, even so, those who survived may have been left with an uneasy feeling of guilt, a need to make atonement to the youth of today for the sacrificed lives of the youth of two generations. When one thinks of the situation in the Middle East, one can see an analogy. Very many people are unable to take a balanced view of the Arab–Israeli conflict because they carry, consciously or unconsciously, a load of guilt about Belsen and the gas-chambers. Nothing, they feel, can be too good for the Jewish nation after what was done to them. Is it so impossible that this kind of guilt may have permeated old–young relationships? Might it not be that we have this feeling that nothing is too good for the children of today because, since 1914, two generations of children have grown up only to become cannon-fodder?

Even if our memories do not stretch back to the First World War, there are other things which we cannot forget which may account for our over-indulgence of the young. Most of us have lived through long periods of deprivation, ranging from the

Hungry Thirties with two million unemployed, means tests, hunger marches, dole queues, to the war with its rationing, blackout, dreariness and discomfort. After the conflict ended there was no let-up and we dragged wearily through further years of austerity. This may seem a silly thing to say, but of the minor discomforts of the war the thing which I hated most was having to eat margarine. By the time butter rationing ended I positively loathed the stuff and swore that I would never again touch it nor have it in the house. I have kept my word although I am quite convinced that, if anyone put me to the test, I should be one of those extraordinary women on T.V. who can't tell Stork from butter!

I truly believe that there are many parents who have such traumatic memories of their own deprived childhoods that they are determined that their children shall have all the happiness and all the little luxuries which poverty or the war denied to them. So often parents of problem children complain that 'they have everything they want—we deny them nothing' (yes, I have actually had this said to me!), and they cannot understand that this indulgence of their children's every whim is the very reason for their problem behaviour. Begin to quote that phrase in any gathering of teachers—'They have everything they want'—and I can guarantee that everyone present will finish it for you: they have *all* heard it, time and time again, and always in the same circumstances.

One of the most tragic things ever told to me was the story of a mother who had gone out to work although her husband had a good job and she did not particularly enjoy working. Her fourteen-year-old daughter, alone in an empty house all through the school holidays, started to bring boy-friends home. It was not long until she was practically running a teenage brothel. When she was pregnant—the father possibly one of many—and the whole thing came to light, the distracted mother said, 'And I only went out to work to get things for her.'

This desire to shower material benefits on the children, springing as I think it may from possible guilt feelings and certainly from recollections of past austerity, is naturally increased by the powerful influences of highly organized commercialism which we have already looked at, and by public confusion and apathy. Even those parents who do not think that their children should have everything they ask for and who resent the pressures of advertising on the young sometimes feel that they are fighting a losing battle, and they fall victim to the importunity of young people's steadily reiterated 'Everyone else is allowed to . . .' or 'Everyone else has . . .' or even 'Everyone else's parents . . .' It is not true, of course, for the plain fact is that 'everyone else's parents' are being subjected to the same kind of blackmail, but it takes a strong-minded parent to reply, 'I don't care what everyone else does, *you* are not going to do it!' And what is more, to mean it and to be prepared to fight the same battle over and over again. I do not happen to believe that those who make a stand for what they believe to be right are losing out; but is it not better, as I said to Rotary, to light one candle than to sit and grumble at the darkness?

Up to now, all the reasons which I have found for adult failure are entirely understandable, and I have a certain amount of sympathy with those who succumb to the many and varied pressures. There is, however, one class of adult for whose motives I have nothing but contempt. These are the people who for obscure and suspect reasons inflate the ego of the teenagers, even to the extent of saying publicly, over and over again, how much they envy them and wish that *they* were still in their teens. I happen to like the music of the Beatles, although I do not feel that they did their generation any service with such songs as 'Lucy in the Sky with Diamonds'. But I fail to understand the mentality of the serious critics who wrote pages analysing their pleasant but ephemeral music and calling them the greatest song-writers since Schubert, or of a Prime Minister who gave them the M.B.E. Is it any wonder that an article should recently have appeared, written by a so-called pop star of whom I admit I have never even heard, in which he seriously states that his music is in every way superior to that of Beethoven, Britten and all serious musicians, past and present?

Elderly dons come out—or should it be sit in?—in sympathy with striking students, much to the annoyance of the students, who do not want to be found dead in the same sit-in as their elders. Ageing M.P.s write to *The Times* urging the legalization of marijuana, or the utter harmlessness of L.S.D. not because *they* want to turn on, but because they feel it incumbent upon them to urge the young to do so. They smile benignly on youthful experimentation with drugs and call it a sign of the free-thinking, healthy independence of the modern generation; they applaud sexual promiscuity as a throwing-off of the shackles of prudery and back up student demands for contraceptives in slot-machines and mixed sleeping-arrangements in hostels.

What can possibly be at the root of this egging-on of the young to do the things which their elders never thought of doing? Is it a rather nasty vicarious pleasure? I sometimes fear that it is, that some people feel a peculiarly twisted envy of the *real* freedoms of the young, freedoms which obviously an older generation did not have for all kinds of reasons, not least the war. Because in their secret hearts they resent and hate the young for having so much that they did not have, they have a subconscious urge to destroy them. Most of us had a perfectly happy childhood and grew up reasonably unresentful of the discipline which our parents exerted over us. A misfit minority were unhappy, and it is they who are urging young people to jump into bed with one another, to rebel, to wear outrageous or even indecent clothes, to experiment with drugs—in short, to do all the things which these sad, middle-aged, frustrated people imagine that they would have liked to do when they were young. And an equally misfit minority of the young takes this poisonous advice and, because they are noisy and exhibitionist, they are regarded as typical of their generation and pressure is brought to bear on the law-abiding majority to imitate them.

The total irresponsibility of some public figures who take it upon themselves to give advice to the young is inexplicable unless one accepts the theory that they are really out to corrupt them; and I would hesitate to assume this of those whom I have in mind.

A few years ago, when I was headmistress of a day school, a well-meaning member of staff recommended for the library some books specially written for teenagers, giving them factual knowledge of sexual matters as well as advice. She had not read the books but they had been well reviewed and were by reputable experts. Before putting them in the library the librarian, a young and very with-it married woman, read them. She brought one to me and asked me whether I thought it was suitable. Both she and her husband, when appealed to for an opinion, had thought that it was not. I read it: the chapter to which they had taken exception began with the assumption, explicit not tacit, that boy and girl readers of the book would wish to experiment with sex. The writer made it fairly obvious that he approved of this, although he did say that they might find it difficult as narrow-minded parents were not likely to put a bed at their disposal and sex could be tricky in a car or behind a hedge. (After this lapse of time, I cannot recall the exact words, but let me assure my readers that I do not exaggerate.) The book then went on to give explicit advice on birth control, while at the same time describing the sex act in erotic language quite unsuited to an allegedly scientific account. The boys and girls were told lyrically of the joys which they might expect, especially if they managed to master the art of *coitus interruptus* and so prolong the physical pleasure almost indefinitely. The author carefully neglected to mention that, if they did not manage to master that rather difficult 'art', they would end up with an unwanted baby. I was so amazed by this book that I felt I must take further advice, so I asked yet another married woman, an older one this time, what *she* thought. She also compared notes with her husband and reported to me that they actually found much of it sexually exciting to read. This then was intended to be placed in the hands of teenagers. I submit that the writer and the publisher were guilty of almost criminal irresponsibility.

It was at about the same time that I was watching a T.V. discussion on the young. Incidentally, my deputy, yet another married woman with a daughter of her own, was so incensed by this programme that she was still simmering with rage the next morning. One of the speakers, whose name is a household word, solemnly advised all parents to see that their teenage daughter had a contraceptive sheath in her handbag when she went out to a dance, presumably to hand to the boy who asked her to have intercourse. (Where? In a car or behind a hedge, presumably. Or would the really with-it parent invite them home and put the spare bedroom at their disposal?) The thing that had so infuriated my deputy was not so much this piece of advice but the fatuous comment of another member of the panel: 'But if the girl didn't have the opportunity to use it, wouldn't she feel *rejected?*'

An article appeared in a national newspaper some little while ago in which the writer solemnly debated what one should do when one's student daughter brought a new boy-friend home for the first time. Would not the realistic thing be to put them together in a double bedroom rather than support the hypocritical pretence that they were not sleeping together?

Yet another example from the Press of giving advice which is just about as lethal as handing a child with a sore throat potassium cyanide to gargle with appeared on the woman's page of a highly reputable Sunday newspaper. It was written by a well-known columnist who, as far as I know, is a happily married woman, and it largely consisted of excellent advice to girls leaving school, either for jobs away from home or for university. Mainly it was advice on how to budget: so much a month for nylons, so much for cosmetics, for hair-dos, as well as for the major items like rent, food, clothes, holidays, etcetera. Then quite casually, and as though it were the most normal thing in the world, one other item figured in this budget for beginners—so much a month for the contraceptive pill.

I sometimes think that I am so square as to be practically cubic, despite the assurance given to the Press by those girls of mine that I am not, but is it really so square not to find it normal and natural that an eighteen-year-old, away from a decent, normal, loving home in an allegedly Christian country, should go immediately on the Pill? Surely, as it has ever been, a minority of youngsters, once on the loose, will sleep around at the earliest possible opportunity, but the majority will not do so unless—and this is the crux of the matter—unless they have been made to think, by articles such as this, that they are in some way unnatural or sexual failures if they do not. I am reminded of the young woman who wrote to tell me that she had been made to feel odd by some members of her college staff simply because she did not 'sleep around', and worried about it until she realized that she was happy in her oddness.

I remember also listening to a B.B.C. interview—I believe it was that excellent programme *Today*—with the teenagers who were taking part in a theatrical venture at, I think, the Royal Court. The young people had done a census and had discovered that something like ninety-eight per cent of them were virgin with every intention of remaining so until they married. The reporter asked them, 'It doesn't look as though you are very permissive, then?' to which came the reply, uttered in derisive tones which cheered my square old heart, 'No, we aren't per-sive. It's just that the grown-ups *expect* us to be permissive.' What a shocking indictment of our craven generation!

The influence of the mass-media on the young is obviously so great that it would need a book all of its own, if one were to explore it thoroughly. Some of the things which I have already said clearly apply to the mass-media. Television panels are too often entirely composed of frightened people who are so mes-merized by the camera and so eager to say not what they really believe but what is currently the with-it thing that one longs to kick them. In the entertainment room beforehand, over drinks and sandwiches, they all reveal themselves as perfectly normal squarish people, with fairly conventional ideas on bringing up the young and reasonably happy families. As soon as the red light goes on they cravenly abdicate, assure one another that, of course, the generation gap is unbridgeable and, naturally, they cannot communicate with their children and, certainly, they would never insist on being obeyed by them. If one member of the panel tries to stick up for the principles which they all professed in private, they turn and rend him in case they should spoil their liberal T.V. image. My mother invented an absol-utely splendid category into which she put the fools and knaves of her acquaintance—'people I should like to pole-axe'. I would say that T.V. panels positively abound with candidates for inclusion.

The growing discussion of violent and sexual scenes on

television is rapidly being drawn into the debate on the whole subject of law and order. It was rather a pity that a paper such as *The Times* treated so serious a matter in such a trivial way, coming to the conclusion that, out of one week's viewing, scenes of sex, violence and swearing took up only one per cent of the viewing-time, for this proves absolutely nothing. There must still be many homes where children do not regularly hear swearing and where, if they swore, they would be reproved. I cannot imagine that very many schools allow children to swear openly. I realize that the whole business of swearing is debatable—after all, *why* should some words be permissible and others not?—but the monotonous repetition of ritual obscenities surely betrays a coarsened mind and blunted imagination. Why then should the swear-word 'bloody' be used forty-seven times in one week on British television? Some programmes—notably *The Dustbinmen* and *Steptoe and Son*—are notoriously foul-mouthed, presenting a level of invective which is quite foreign to most of the people in this country. I am not trying to pretend that I never let rip with some unparliamentary language on occasion but I draw the line, *and so should the B.B.C.*, at the following, all heard repeatedly during the six days 31 March to 5 April 1970, by the *Times* research team: 'Get stuffed; bum; Jesus; bastard; bleeding; for Christ's sake; Jesus Christ; sod her; cow; up yours; buggered.' All in addition to the forty-seven 'bloodies'!

The amount of torture, mayhem and murder, both actual and fictional, which is shown on T.V. is very disturbing indeed. In the same few days *The Times* reports killing by pistol, rifle, sword, spear, knife, arrow and blunt instrument, radiation, trident, marauding gorilla, bubonic plague, cyanide and crucifixion. There were also men thrown from a flying aircraft and a high window, one was killed with a scythe, another with a motor-cycle. Whether all this, plus the brutal fighting and the torture, really has any effect on the young, I am not prepared to say. I read and enjoyed horrific tales by the Brothers Grimm and Hans Andersen and in my teens saw the occasional horror film about vampires and monsters and I do not remember being much affected by them. Certainly I do not feel that they have brutalized me in any way and I sometimes think that children are tougher than we imagine. Nevertheless, one feels that there should be subjects more worthy of display on the small screen than this perpetual parade of death in all its more beastly forms.

The *Times* finding was that scenes involving physical sex were extremely unusual. This is obviously so, since there is still, one assumes, some sort of internal censorship which would forbid the filming of actual intercourse. I suppose that the nearest the B.B.C. has come to it was in Ken Russell's tasteless film about Richard Strauss, which I thought silly as well as nasty.

I am not especially worried about the occasional bed with a man's naked back and a girl's naked shoulders. I find more amusing than anything else the extraordinary convention, chiefly seen in American films of a few years back, that women make love in their petticoats and men in their trousers but not their shirts! Unless we are always to assume that they have just got up and modestly resumed their trousers! What I do object to very much indeed—and this is where I think television is much to be blamed—is the totally unnecessary injection of promiscuous or at any rate extra-marital sex into so many programmes. If the story is specifically concerned with the relations of a man with a woman, then of course there may be scenes with an erotic content, if these are vital to the development of the plot and character. I can see no point at all in deliberately and for no ascertainable reason, other than a desire to titillate, introducing erotic scenes into such programmes as *Doomwatch* and *Special Branch*. In a recent episode we were shown one of the *Doomwatch* team in an extremely sexual scene with a girl-friend and, just to add a bit of spice to the encounter, she was coloured. What this had to do with an investigation into pollution of rivers was not made clear. Similarly, in an episode of *Special Branch*, the detective was telephoned by his boss with an assignment. The call found him naked in bed with a naked girl. Just in case we missed the point, the camera had itself a ball, dodging all around him as he got out of bed and dressed, managing somehow to give an impression of complete nudity while never actually revealing all. As a sort of highly erotic male strip-tease in reverse it was a great success, but I fail to see its

73

relevance to the plot, which had something to do with espionage and did not in any way involve his bed-mate, whom we never saw again.

One gets the distinct impression that nearly all of T.V. starts from the tacit assumption that chastity before and fidelity within marriage are absolutely outworn conventions and that every normal man and woman will, at some point in a normal working day, drop everything (literally and figuratively) in order to have sexual intercourse with whoever happens to be around at the time. Maybe the world of the T.V. producer is like this, but I cannot see that it is relevant to the experience of most people, and it is not the sort of image that we should be projecting into the minds of young people. I have found the comments of many of my married friends on this subject very significant. Both men and women have told me that they find it acutely embarrassing to sit through explicitly sexual scenes in the presence of their marriage partner. Lest the Freudians leap on this with cries of 'Complex!' these are people who are normally broad-minded and who make no secret of the fact that their intimate lives are extremely happy. Perhaps because of this, they have no wish to watch something which is precious and private to them used as public entertainment.

Do we, as parents, as teachers, as directors of the B.B.C. and I.T.V., really *believe* that it is in the best interests of society that a climate of opinion should gradually be built up in which promiscuous sex, with all its concomitant factors of illegitimacy and venereal disease, should become the accepted norm? If we do not, then it is time that we stopped cheapening and trivializing the sexual relationship by treating it so casually and contemptuously.

When one turns to the cinema there is an equally depressing tale to tell. I used to be a very keen cinema-goer, but I have not seen a film for three years and in the two years before that I think I saw two. Time was when whole families went to the 'pictures', but when is there anything now to which one could take the family? Out of twenty-five London cinemas advertising in *The Times* in a recent week ten had X-certificate films. This does not take into account the hosts of near-pornographic films with X-certificates which are not advertised but which one seems to see at every street corner in London. The West End gets more like 42nd Street every week. Maybe young people do not go to see these films, although I am sure that many of them do, but they know that they are *there*, their imagination is caught by hearing about them and so the cheapening and coarsening process continues. Do we really want our children to grow up to be a nation of *voyeurs* with nothing better to do than to watch other people having sex? Perhaps *The Day of the Sex Olympics* is nearer than we think?

The great mass of the population do not want these films and do not go to see them (which is why cinemas are turning to bingo), and yet they continue to be made. If their directors, producers and actors enjoy this sort of mutual masturbation, well and good, but I cannot see why they should be paid to do it or why anyone should pretend that the films have anything to with (a) art or (b) entertainment.

When I was a student I used to long for the day when I should be able to afford to buy books, other than the ones which I needed for my studies. Now that I have money to spend, I suppose I buy about one book a year. Most of the non-fiction that I want to read I do not particularly want to keep, and, if I do, it will probably be in the school reference library. I read fewer and fewer novels each year and buy hardly any. There are perhaps three serious novelists whose books I look forward to, buy, and read over and over again. Each week I assiduously study the reviews, only to decide yet again that there is nothing at all that I have the slightest desire to read. What is more, almost everyone with whom I am in touch feels much the same, and I suppose that my acquaintance is fairly literate.

Most readers nowadays simply say that they never read novels, others that they have *given up* reading novels. The libraries are full of disconsolate people prowling around the shelves, complaining that it gets harder and harder to find anything to read. More and more people are falling back on the classics because they find modern novels unreadable. The complaint is made that young people do not read. Is anyone surprised when there is so little that a concerned adult can

75

recommend to them? I personally am sick to death of the anti-hero, spelling out his sex life in four-letter words in some sleazy bed-sitter. I am also very tired of the many incompetent imitators of Ian Fleming who interrupt the action of their story on every other page in order that the hero may copulate. Sex is becoming one colossal bore, and one really wonders why any writer should want to spend weeks and months writing detailed descriptions of the sexual gymnastics of a couple in bed, which is practically all there was in the latest novel by one well-known woman writer. The *Khama Sutra* has done it much better, anyway.

Even books which manage very well without sex on every page now seem to need sex on the cover if they are to sell in paperback. Once, Penguin books were immediately recognizable by the familiar plain cover in orange or green. Not any more—Penguins have discovered sex in all its glory. I have rarely seen anything nastier (or less relevant to the novels) than the paperback covers on a set of three thrillers which they published last year. The naked body of a girl appears to be tattooed all over but the immediate impression is that she is in the last stages of some loathsome and disfiguring skin disease. I read all three novels when they were first published and two of them are good. I could not bear to have them on my shelves in their present covers. Look along the shelves in any paperback bookshop and you will think that it is concerned almost solely with hard-core pornography. This is not the case on the whole, and it would be difficult even to find copies of *Last Exit to Brooklyn.* Why is it thought desirable to disguise even the most harmless author in covers portraying quite revolting violence— I saw one the other day of a naked belly with a knife twisted in a pretty repulsive wound—or else naked bodies? A combination of the two seems to be a sure-fire seller.

It may be thought that I am galloping off on a hobby-horse and getting away from the subject in hand, but this *is* the subject in hand, the whole rotten world that *we* have created for our children. Because *they* do not write the sexy books, the T.V. or film scripts, *they* are not behind the cameras of the near-blue films, nor do they design suggestive book-jackets in order to gull the prurient into buying. Teenagers buy in thousands the books of the few writers who are not ashamed to tell a good story, yet adult critics never miss a chance to sneer at such writers as 'best-sellers', and even to laugh at the decency of the characters in them.

One of the very few writers whom I do buy, not only because of the spell-binding nature of the story-telling which keeps one turning the pages until the end but also because of the blessedly literate style and magnificent evocation of atmosphere, sells in millions of copies in almost every country in the world. This writer's women readers complain that as soon as a new book comes into the house it is monopolized first by the husband and then by all the teenagers. Yet there is always some critic who sneers at these books for the simple reason that the action is not continually interrupted for sexual athletics. One such critic wonderingly remarked that he could not understand why these books sold in millions, when the standards which the writer believed in no longer existed. It did not seem to occur to him that, although these standards—of honour, courage, chastity— might have ceased to exist for him, millions of ordinary folk all over the world were still trying to live by them and, what is more important, to bring up their children by them.

Why *should* those of us who happen to think that there is still room in the world for truth, gentleness and consideration, for responsibility, for service and, above all, for love, be treated as simple-minded fools, living in a romantic dream? These writers and critics, these manipulators of the mass media, try to justify their preoccupation with the sexy and sordid by saying that this is 'real life' and that it is cowardly or escapist to portray anything else. What they seem to ignore is that there is another side to life as well and that it is equally cowardly and escapist to pretend that nothing exists that is true, honest, just, pure, lovely and of good report. Is there any good reason why we should not at least try to teach our children to think on these things?

6

The Rights of the Young

Many of the rebel students who storm into the administration buildings of their universities assert that they are only demanding their rights. I never feel that anyone is on very firm ground when he begins to talk about 'rights' because, when that happens, someone else is just as likely to start to demand his, and too often the rights cancel one another out, two rights managing to make a wrong! If A is to have his rights, then B cannot have his, and who has the better right to his rights? Nevertheless, I do believe that young people (and here I am thinking more of children of school age than of the student fraternity) have an absolute right to expect certain things to be provided for them by their elders. I do not believe that children should have to be grateful for this provision, for gratitude can be a most corrosive thing, well calculated to erode any relationship. Parents too often complain that they have done everything for their children, have even made sacrifices for them, and have received nothing in return. I cannot see that they should expect anything other than their children's love, and not even that if all they have given are material things. People who complain that no one loves them rarely stop to ask whether they are indeed lovable.

The first and probably the most important absolute right of a child is the right to security. This is a basic and fundamental need and it has nothing at all to do with a lavish provision of material things for it cannot be bought with money. We have all known homes where this world's goods were very short but where there was such an atmosphere of love and trust that the children were rich indeed.

To provide this security demands very real and strenuous self-sacrifice on the part of the parents, and a strong purpose, for it has its roots in *their* integrity. Standards must be set high and maintained at all costs, not only in order to set a good example to the young but also because these standards are right in themselves. It is useless to expect your child to tell you the truth if you lie to him or to trust you if you break your promises or to be honest if he sees you cheating, even in what may seem trivial ways. At no time must standards be lowered for the sake of courting popularity. It is sometimes the case that one parent will countermand the orders of the other, simply to curry favour with the children. Nothing is more destructive of peace in the home and the net result is that the children grow up in total confusion of what is right and wrong.

There must be agreement between parents as to what the rules are and under no circumstances must they let each other down by 'unilateral disarmament'. It may be trite but it is very true that example is better than precept, and the children must know that the whole household is ruled by right principles, not by unreasonable whims or temporary moods. A teenager will almost certainly question his parents' standards and he may choose to depart from them, but he must be confronted daily by their steady influence or he will have the greatest difficulty in ever finding the security of having standards at all.

There seems to be an almost universal conspiracy to talk absolute nonsense about the young so that ultimately it becomes the accepted orthodoxy. One of the greatest pieces of nonsense is the idea that the revolt of the young against authority is the result of too rigid discipline in their formative years. I cannot see that this is true since this is the generation that has not been disciplined, that has never met the challenge of adult authority and is therefore being driven to one extreme after another, almost as though they were daring adults to stand up to them. Discipline *is* the teaching of standards—after all, it comes from the Latin verb 'to learn'. It has nothing to do with corporal punishment, the writing of lines, detentions and all the petty punishments of certain schools, now few and far between.

It is useless to prate of 'self-discipline' as if it were an innate quality with which every baby is born. Self-discipline is the ultimate end of discipline: the grown man's integrity is proof against all assaults, he holds fast to that which is good because nothing less satisfies him, but this state cannot be achieved without guidance. I wonder if anyone reads Proverbs nowadays?

79

There is much to be said for the following: 'Observe, O my son, the commandment of your father, and do not forsake the law of your mother. Tie them upon your heart constantly; bind them upon your throat. When you walk about, it will lead you; when you lie down, it will stand guard over you; and when you have waked up, it itself will make you its concern. For the commandment is a lamp, and a light the law is, and the reproofs of discipline are the way of life.'

A family is a community, and any community has the right to ask its members to develop within the framework of discipline which is the logical necessity of the community's existence. If one accepts the privileges and protection of belonging to a community, then one obeys its rules. Neither do I believe that a community of young and old such as a family or even a school can be a democracy. I agree with the authors of the American study *Teenage Tyranny* that: 'We ask young people too often what they think we should do about them. By telling them that this is the democratic way, we not only make them believe it is wrong for adults to impose standards and set some rules and limitations, but we deprive them of meaningful guidance.'

I have been in charge of teenage girls for twenty years, first as deputy head of co-educational schools and then as a head-mistress. My basic attitude to the setting of standards has not changed in those years because, though one varies the letter of the law, it is the same spirit which one interprets to different generations. When a girl questions a rule I always make it abundantly clear that, *in the first place*, she obeys it because I say so, and that if she wants the kind of education which the school gives, then she accepts my right to make the rules since I, not she, am accountable to others for what goes on in the school. Nevertheless, I then see that she fully understands the reason for the rule which she is questioning, and I am always prepared to discuss it with her and even to change the rule if she can convince me that she is right and I am wrong.

I am quite prepared to be vigorously attacked by the progressives for this maternalistic insistence that I am the 'boss': all I can say is that it *works*. Of course, no child should be bullied or beaten or, at the other extreme, over-protected, but so long as he is dependent for food, shelter, clothing, education—in short, for everything—on his parents and teachers, then his part of the bargain is to do as they tell him. The responsibility of the adults is to see that he understands why they tell him so and if there is mutual trust, love and respect he will accept this situation.

I have said that I am always prepared to discuss reasons with my pupils. This takes time, but it is time that must be taken, for it is well spent and there is no substitute for it. It is even more essential in the family situation where disagreements can be much more fundamental and therefore much more bitter than in school. Generous presents and holidays abroad are no substitute for personal attention, and parents must see that both of them have time for listening without distraction, for considered judgement, patient explanation and unruffled repetition. Many of the problems which arise at school and in play may seem silly and trivial to the adult but they loom very large in the child's mind and he must be able to pour them out to an attentive ear. If you do not listen to him, you will one day find that he has ceased to talk to you.

Love is the basis of security, not sentimentality or indulgence. It must be guaranteed and inexhaustible but it must deny as well as give; denounce as well as condone; demand as well as provide. Let our children be aware of our love and concern for them, not by the lavishness of the gifts which we shower upon them nor by the freedom to please themselves which we give them, but by the exercise of a kind but firm authority which will protect them from their own follies and inexperience. Shakespeare was not far wrong when he said in *Antony and Cleopatra*:

> We, ignorant of ourselves,
> Beg often our own harms, which the wise powers
> Deny us for our good: so find we profit
> By losing of our prayers.

If we love our children, then we shall give some careful thought to their choice of companions. Children do not appreciate the seriousness of bad associations, but parents should. This is a very difficult problem, and it is simply not possible to lay down hard and fast rules; for, obviously, if a friendship of which one disapproves has become really deep-rooted, forbidding it will only make matters worse. This is one of those cases where parents need to have second sight; they must not only see life steadily and see it whole, they must also see it coming! There are usually subtle methods of easing a child out of a potentially dangerous association before any harm is done or any close links forged, providing one is sufficiently interested to know always who the child's friends are. When children get into serious trouble it is extraordinary how little the parents often know about where they have been or with whom. Many a time they have not even asked. I should have thought that 'Where are you going and who are you going with?' was the essential question which every parent would be sure to ask.

In an earlier chapter I quoted at some length from the letter of an old-age pensioner. I should like to come back to him now:

> Today the father has his car that's his image. The mother goes out to work and then to bingo or the pubs in their cars with work-mates. They buy their children prams and bikes and give them a lot of pocket-money and let them run wild at all hours instead of growing up with them at home and teaching them guidance in doing the right or wrong things in life. This I have proved with my own, not forgetting we came from the slums of London, if we can do it with patience and tolerance and plenty of love and affection, it can be done with happy results.

As children enter the teens, parents can unwittingly expose them to moral dangers which the young people themselves may recognize but find difficulty in resisting. I am going to state with all the force and conviction that I can muster that any parents who hand over their homes to teenagers for unsupervised parties must be mentally unbalanced or criminally irresponsible. However innocently these parties may begin, there is always the danger of gate-crashers—some parents have returned to find distracted children trying to set to rights a vandalized home with no redress because they did not even know who the vandals were. Some silly boy may think it clever or daring to bring drink to the party, even to 'spike' the coke with gin or vodka. If this occurs, the least that can happen will be that some youngsters will be very sick on your drawing-room carpet. Sooner or later, the lights will go out and sexual feelings will be aroused, the strength of which the young do not anticipate. I have actually known parents to go away from home for the whole night, sleeping at the house of friends while their teenage children threw an all-night party. Not only is it absolute madness to allow that sort of party in one's own house, it is just as important to see that one's children do not go to them in other people's houses. Here again, it is essential to know who the friends are and what the standards of their parents are.

In one extremely happy family which I know, the daughter is never allowed to spend the night at the homes of the party-givers but is collected at a reasonable hour, either by Father's car or by taxi. At first she was inclined to resent this, but after a few parties she actually told her father that she was glad. Sometimes, she said, the parties got 'a bit draggy' or she got stuck with a boy who was 'a bit of a creep', and it was a relief to have an excuse to go home and to be able to put the blame on Father!

I had a somewhat similar situation in my school. The sixth form were invited to a dance to which they did not particularly want to go. Any adult would simply have refused gracefully but they were concerned lest they should seem rude or priggish. (They had not much liked the behaviour of the boys at the last similar dance!) Their faces lit up when I cheerfully told them that they could not go in any case because it was too near to exams, not an exeat day and they had work to do.

'Don't you mind if we put the blame on you?' they asked.

'Not a bit,' I answered. 'That's one of the things I'm here for!'

Parents are asking for trouble if they do not keep an unobtrusive eye on the places which the young frequent: the coffee-bar, discothèque, bowling-alley, even the youth club. Vigilance can be maintained without the children feeling that they are being spied upon, but it is important to be sure, or at least as sure as one can be, that these places are not being used for the peddling of drugs or pornography.

There comes a time when the young want to spread their

wings a little and have a holiday away from the family. This again is a tricky problem and much depends on the individual child. On the whole, however, I think that it is most unwise to allow girl- and boy-friend to go off unaccompanied or in a foursome with another couple on camping and hitch-hiking holidays. There are many organizations which cater for young people—pony-trekking, rock-climbing, all kinds of outdoor activities, with proper supervision and not many opportunities for romantic pairing-off. These could very well satisfy the adolescent's craving for independence without putting him at risk.

Of course, for family life to be truly satisfying, more is needed than just avoiding what is harmful. There should be the enjoyment of doing things together as a family, for the real joy of family life is lost when each one goes his own way without regard for the others. When there is real family discussion, when plans are laid together and everyone works together to fulfil them, the family is drawn together in real unity. There should be more for a family to do together than watch T.V.

Security and love: the twin supports of the happy family in which a child can be free to develop his personality—his next essential right. At no time of life is the individual so conscious of separate identity and of personal uniqueness as during the teens. The complaint is often heard that young people are entirely selfish: this is something which parents ought to be prepared for since a profound interest in, and sensitivity towards, self is absolutely characteristic of the teens. Young people—and this applies very much to the student age-group as well as to the teenagers—are vitally concerned about themselves and their relationships. The questions that loom largest in their minds are questions of identity: who am I? What sort of a person am I? What is going to happen to *me*?

It is tremendously important to realize the sheer *physical* turmoil that is going on inside the body of the adolescent and the effect which this is bound to have on the developing personality. Many children are intelligent enough to recognize the signs of stress and turmoil in themselves and others and even to laugh, albeit ruefully, at their erratic behaviour. If parents

84

and teachers take the trouble to prepare the young for the peaks of elation and troughs of depression in which they will alternately find themselves during the perilous journey through the teens, much strife, misunderstanding and misery may be saved on both sides.

Not so long ago I held a conference between myself, those of my staff most concerned with a certain age-group in school and the girls themselves, in an effort to find out just why some of the latter had been particularly 'bolshy' that term. One or two genuine grievances came to light and were remedied, and the mere fact of talking about the problem went a long way to solving it, so that the rest of the term was comparatively trouble-free. As the meeting was breaking up with everyone feeling that a good understanding had been reached, I was immensely cheered and more than a little amused at being told in kindly tones by one girl, 'You mustn't worry, Miss Manners, it's only our age, you know.'

This right to discover one's own personality, almost to come to grips with the psychology of man himself, must never be usurped by parents and teachers. This is where we must walk the incredibly difficult path of guidance which will nevertheless give a child the opportunity to explore values and conduct, to test his beliefs and to examine his faith, to discover what his real thoughts, feelings and needs are. Self-awareness and self-determination need to be established gradually, and the process must be well on its way by the time a boy or girl has left school.

It was recently put to me by a university counsellor that many of the drop-outs from university should never have been there in the first place but had been fed into the conveyor-belt system by parents and teachers who had never given them the chance to discover whether they themselves actually wanted to spend three or four years studying for a degree. Once at university and freed from the influence of the adults who for years have virtually usurped their lives, these young people begin to experience a sort of eleventh-hour awareness and realize for the first time that they have not the slightest desire to be where they are. One wonders whether some at least of students' rebellion may not be caused by those who, having come to the university without any genuine personal motivation, but merely because it was expected of them, now express their frustration by trying to destroy the institution into which they cannot fit. Even if it were desirable, we cannot *impose* our own value-system on the young. We can only hope that the steady influence of standards believed in, adhered to and increasingly seen to bring the stay of a good conscience, will in the event have its effect. But in a world which, as we have seen, is infinitely more complex, where the rate of change is greater, where the certainties which we enjoyed are gone and where authority-figures cut less and less ice, we cannot merely take an authoritarian line and live our children's lives for them.

Overprotectiveness in childhood can equally result in disaster in young adulthood. There is a world of difference between armouring a child against all the wiles of the Devil and never letting him be aware that the Devil exists and, moreover, that he has many devoted and enthusiastic followers. A young woman from a home where a kind of fundamentalist religion is still being preached (and they do exist even in this day and age), who has been brought up to believe implicitly in the old right and wrong of the hell-fire evangelist, who has never been given any opportunity to take out her values and, as it were, look at them, is in grave danger of having her whole scale of values seriously undermined when she comes in contact with the profane old world. Overwhelmed and confused by the behaviour of others, of which her strictly religious upbringing has given her no inkling, guilty at her inability to live up to her 'own' standards (without realizing that they never were her own but had been imposed upon her by her parents and teachers), such a girl may very well throw the whole of her former training overboard in a desperate effort to reassert her own will and discover her own identity.

Throughout the teens and early twenties young people have the right to be able to establish meaningful relationships with their elders; they must be able to find adults who are prepared to relate to them in depth. The young people who are growing up happily through the various stages of infancy and youth are those who have found these essential contacts with their own parents and later with their teachers and, thank goodness, they are still in the majority. But there has obviously been something seriously *wrong* in the relationships of any young man, intelligent enough to get a university place in these days of fierce competition, who can seriously talk about the 'suffocating bosom of the elder generation'. Nothing is more calculated to drive the young into isolation and a slavish adherence to group opinion within their own sub-culture than the suspicion and antagonism born of this failure to establish a proper relationship with older people. And as I have already said, this desperate desire to belong is probably the most serious threat to the development of personality which the young have to face. Ironically enough, this dangerous conformity is in many ways in direct conflict with their real desires, for they do not really want to be nothing but one of a crowd, at an age when they desperately desire to be themselves alone.

Recently, the *Times Educational Supplement* had a competition for young writers, the subject to be a school story. Many of the most impressive and touching entries came from young people who wrote of the loneliness and isolation, the awfulness of being different at school, and yet what came through very clearly was their passionate assertion of the right, indeed the *need*, to be different. One wrote of the boy 'who had entered a vicious circle. The more he tried to be accepted, the more awkward he became and the more he was rejected.' Finally 'his mask of indifference became reality. It was now he understood the futility of his existence. But he had conformed.' Another wrote of a girl who says, 'I'm easily led. I do a lot of things that everyone else does—I smoke, I swear, I wear those ghastly black skirts. Protesting is such an old thing now that everybody does it. I'm just a typical English sixteen-year-old girl and there are a million others like me. There is one thing about me though that is different—I mind, I mind, I mind the fact that I have a million twins.'

If only adults would realize that this girl is not different, that indeed the greatest need of all young people is to assert their individuality and that, if only they could be given the help which they have every right to expect but do not always get, they would not conform in this sheep-like way to an image which they secretly resent and despise.

So far the rights which I have discussed have all been somewhat intangible things, but I should like to touch briefly on one other right that one would not expect to find challenged in the world today: namely, the right to education. It is a source of constant amazement to me that there are still parents, in all social classes, who actively prevent their sons—and, more often, their daughters—from continuing with their education for as long as they can benefit from it. Parents who would never dream of arguing with a doctor over the best treatment for their child's body frequently stubbornly refuse to be advised by the professionals—the teachers—in the matter of the child's mind.

In the many years which I spent in State schools I was frequently confronted with parents whose attitude to their young was unbelievably selfish and stupid. It began when the girl was approaching the age of fifteen and so, despite the fact that the parents had signed a legal agreement to keep her at grammar school until she was sixteen, could leave school. Far too many parents, rather than cope with her restlessness and unwillingness to do homework when her friends in other types of school were leaving school and getting jobs, would make all sorts of specious excuses for taking her away. It was in this sort of situation that one saw the cowardly abdication of the parents from their responsibility, for over and over again one heard the parrot-cry: 'We only want her to be happy, she must make up her own mind.' Useless to assure them that if only they would make it clear to the girl that agreements are not made to be broken, that she had the ability to go further than a job in a factory or shop and that they intended her to stay at school until she got her 'O' levels, she would get over this bad patch and settle happily, with the rest of her form, to work. It was too much trouble to put up, even temporarily, with her tears and sulks and, in any case, they were clearly pleased at the prospect of having another wage-earner in the house.

More often than not these girls—the 'early leavers' as they are called in the schools—became delinquent, for they were innately too intelligent to be happy in the sort of blind-alley jobs available to them at fifteen without 'O' levels, and so they drifted from one job to another, neither fish, flesh nor good red herring as the saying goes, until eventually they were either in trouble with the police or else pregnant.

Every headmistress could tell stories of the battles which she has fought for girls who have wanted to stay on into the sixth form but whose parents have not seen the point of it, or for girls who have been kept at home at a vital stage in their school careers to shoulder their parents' responsibility for younger children. I have even known a doctor, who should certainly have known better, write a medical certificate stating that a girl was unable to attend school because she was looking after her sick mother. This was, of course, easier for him than trying to make proper arrangements for the care of his patient. The frustration and resentment of that girl against her parents was a frightening thing. Parents have sometimes said to me in these circumstances, 'But what else could we do?' to which my answer has always been, 'Whatever you would have done if you had not had your daughter.' I remember one highly intelligent girl who was kept at home for the last half-term before her 'A' levels in order to cook, clean and wash for her father and brothers while the mother was in hospital. By a miracle she got a university place, but was almost in a state of collapse by the time the examinations were over. It is not to be wondered at that as soon as she was self-supporting financially she removed herself from the parental home and never went back.

Even before the universities got themselves a bad name because of student violence many parents had to be persuaded to allow their children to go there, and I often had great difficulty in getting permission for a girl to apply to any university other than the one in her home town. One girl who actually won an open scholarship to a major university was not allowed to take it up because her parents insisted on her remaining at home. She came to me in despair after a few weeks of her first term, saying that she could not work for they were always interrupting her, and if she stayed at the university after five o'clock there was an argument about where she had been. She, too, quietly removed herself from home altogether as soon as she had the courage to do so, and now is totally estranged from her parents, having committed the cardinal crime of marrying a man of another religion. This was the very thing which the parents had most feared and was the reason why they had tried to thwart her desire for higher education. It is hardly surprising that her rebellion against their selfishness had the result it did.

A professor of Hull University once told me of a brilliant young freshman who came to him in distress early in his first term, saying that he would have to go home and give up any thought of a university course. On investigation it turned out that he had received daily letters from his mother, begging him to return, because 'the house is like a tomb, I can do nothing but cry and the dog won't eat'. It hardly seems possible that such parents should exist but they do indeed. With people such as these either bullying, or else indulging, coddling, drowning their children in smother-love, frustrating their legitimate aims or encouraging them in their temporary whims, is it any wonder that we have a minority of rebellious, delinquent young people, anxious to break away as soon as possible from the stifling atmosphere of the home?

Even when one deals with parents who are better educated, it is surprising how often one meets opposition to the child's education. Suggest that a girl might profitably read mathematics or physics and they will look alarmed and suggest a nice secretarial or Cordon Bleu course at a good finishing-school. Mention the sixth form and 'A' levels and you are told that they think she would do better in a more 'relaxed' atmosphere. Far too often they write to you suggesting that she should drop half her subjects 'because she isn't really interested and won't need them when she leaves school'. I once taught a girl who really had a burning desire to become a teacher but was afraid to tell her parents so. When *I* told them, their reaction was comical. 'We always hoped she would do something *normal*,' they said.

It will be a national tragedy if the law-and-order backlash actually does result in parents' becoming even more suspicious of education than some of them already are. Some of the current rejection of authority may stem in part from the widening gap in knowledge between the generations. We are educating children for a future unimaginably strange, and the old and middle-aged are finding themselves left behind, especially those who have the extra handicap of never having had adequate education in their own youth. If parents react to this changing situation with jealousy and resentment and try to stop the process by hindering the education of their children, a truly alarming conflict will develop. Even where families have few intellectual interests in common as a result of the 'education gap', there is generally a bond of natural affection—a strong bond but not one that can take every strain. Parents must beware lest they weaken it by trying to hold their children back and by begrudging them the education which they have every right to expect, for under that kind of strain the bond will snap.

It is in this kind of difficult situation that parents and teachers can most help each other, for the teacher still preserves some status with the half-educated young as a person who knows, or at least is interested in knowing. The more parents and teachers can get together on friendly and natural terms, the better. Parents sometimes feel envy because teenagers talk more freely to teachers than to them. This may occur because teachers are emotionally uninvolved but also because they are considered by the young to know something in a world where knowledge counts. If it is not to be a world where the generations line up on opposite sides, all adults must help one another to bridge the gap, parents and teachers most of all since they alone have close and continuous access to young people in the daily routines of home and school from the earliest years.

They are the people who must join forces in the battle to secure the inalienable rights of the young. They should stop sniping at each other, for they are, or should be, all on the same side. Let us hear less of 'What are the parents doing to let this happen?' and 'Why aren't the schools doing more about it?' Let them fight together against the debased standards which adult society allows itself at the same time as it calls for higher ones among the younger generation.

7

The Responsibilities of the Young

Let us assume for the sake of argument that our young people have been given these rights and therefore have no particular cause for complaint against their elders. Generally speaking, I think that this may very well be the case with the great majority of the young. It seems a pity that five per cent of the population gets ninety-five per cent of the publicity. What then are the responsibilities which the young may reasonably be expected to accept, what principles of conduct should we ask of them?

First, I can only repeat what I have said already: that, providing adults are keeping their side of the bargain, the young should keep theirs, which means accepting the *reasonable* authority of those who provide them with everything which they have. Once a young man is earning his own living and is in no way dependent on parents or tax-payers, then he may expect to take a *full* share in the decision-making process of the community to which he is making his own contribution. But schoolchildren and university students must surely see that they are apprentices, not masters, and that just as their responsibility—their accountability—*for* and to the community is limited and their dependence *on* the community practically unlimited, so their rights within that community must be somewhat less than those of 'fully paid-up members'.

This seems to me such obvious justice and common sense that I cannot see how any reasonable youngster can quarrel with it. The freedom to develop can never be the freedom to do as one likes, and I cannot emphasize too strongly that this freedom must be enjoyed within a framework of discipline. The rebellious young too often have a completely unbalanced approach to the whole vexed question of freedom and responsibility. One of the things which every adult learns is that he has frequently to make decisions of importance, decisions which do not only affect himself but can have far-reaching consequences for many other people. This is so obvious that one hardly needs to elaborate it, but let us look at a few simple examples.

The 'job' of a child or young person is usually his school work. If he decides to change his job and opt for German instead of Latin, Chemistry instead of Art, or even if he decides that he would do better at a different school, these decisions will not even ripple the surface of the school. But should his father decide on a change of job, this could have incalculable effects on the lives of his wife and family, for he is responsible for them and any change in his circumstances will affect theirs too. Therefore, he must take into account the consequences of his action before he decides fully to take it. In the same way, no head of a school will lightly embark on a new policy for that school before thoroughly weighing up the pros and cons, since he knows that any change of policy will affect the lives, the happiness, even the future careers of the pupils, perhaps too of the teachers for whom he is responsible.

If young people demand the right to take decisions on matters of importance, then they must be prepared to shoulder the responsibility for the consequences, especially if anything goes wrong as a result. I have a distinct impression that, for all their wild and woolly theorizing, many young militants would be extremely unwilling to accept such a charge. I intend to look much more closely into the question of student and pupil-power in a later chapter. At this point I shall do no more than make the point that I steadfastly deny to anyone who is still at the stage of taking from and not of giving to the community, who moreover cannot, by the very nature of his position in that community, take full responsibility for the consequences of his decisions, the right to *dictate*, by violence if necessary, what the rules must be, thereby over-riding the paramount rights of those who, being the creators and sustainers of that community, bear the greatest responsibility for its continuing well-being.

There was probably never a time in the history of the world when honesty was of more importance than it is now, for the whole of our society is riddled with dishonesty and we are all the poorer for it. It goes without saying that if we are to be able to inculcate the habit of honesty in our children—and we must, for it is one of the basic responsibilities which we must expect from them—then we ourselves must look to our own behaviour. I remember a certain teacher who had caught almost the whole class cheating in examinations. When she tackled them with it one of them answered, 'Father cheats in his income-tax so why shouldn't we cheat in exams?'

It is impossible to make too often or too strongly this point of personal example. There are no better places than the home and school in which to show children the impoverishing effects of lying to each other: how both sides are left with a feeling of degradation. Respect for personal property can and must be taught in the small communities of home and school if it is to persist in the wider world of adult life. From the very earliest age children should not be allowed to get away with lies and unauthorized 'borrowing', and from this kind of personal honesty it should be possible to build up an appreciation of the disastrous effects of dishonesty on a larger scale. Much of the high-powered advertising which children see every day is fundamentally dishonest, for very few commodities live up to their manufacturer's extravagant claims. The shoddy workmanship which renders high-priced goods useless in a short time is an expensive form of dishonesty, and it is obviously essential that young voters should be able to distinguish between the genuine sincerity of some politicians—alas! all too few—and the blatant dishonesty of others. The very fact that the adult world is so full of tricksters masquerading as honest men makes it all the more vital that we should inculcate and expect honesty in our children, in the hope that when *they* are the leaders of society things may be a little better.

I hope that what I have said about the impracticality of handing over decision-making to the young will not be interpreted as meaning that I do not wish them to be given a responsibility at all, for I have already indicated that every child *must* be given responsibility as soon as possible. No one can escape some responsibility for the whole of the group within which he lives, and one of the marks of the adult is that he is, or should be, capable of making responsible decisions and of facing their consequences. Before the young adult reaches an age when he has to exercise his personal responsibility in larger issues and perhaps impersonal groups, he must be allowed to study and practise this difficult technique in the smaller, more personal groups of home and school, where he can actually see the results of his decisions and even of his failure of responsibility. Every possible effort must be made to see that his membership of the community is significant. This is all the more important in schools which are getting bigger and bigger and homes which are in danger of becoming nothing more than filling-stations by day and dormitories by night. Our children must be given a feeling of involvement and a degree of decision-making which is practical. They must be given responsibility, yet we must not be dismayed if they are irresponsible. Particularly, we must not then take their responsibility from them, for if it is their right to be given it, it is their duty to accept it, and we must not lose patience and take over the responsibility ourselves because they have done badly. We must indeed so arrange things that they can learn from their irresponsibilities.

Above all, we must not allow them to opt out of their responsibilities, even though it sometimes means that we have to do some 'nagging'. Every teacher is familiar with the quiet child who shuns the limelight and is convinced that he cannot do the job that he is asked to do. It is only by exercising responsibility that one becomes responsible. There would be less trouble in the universities now if the silent majority would speak up. They too have a stake in the life of the community, and they are as irresponsible as the troublemakers if they do nothing to make their views known, and so allow the militants to have it all their own way.

The trouble about larger and larger schools and enormous sixth forms is that it becomes increasingly difficult to find meaningful posts of responsibility for everyone. It is no answer to the problem to fall back on permissiveness. You do not satisfy a young man's desire for status in the community merely by allowing him to grow his hair and to smoke in the sixth form common-room. Neither is he going to be much interested in the

95

job of collecting the dinner tickets or looking after lost property. After all, if he were not still at school, he would be earning his living, he might even have a wife and child. Unless we evolve really meaningful functions for the older pupils in our schools and the older members of our families, they will be bored and resentful of their subordinate position. By encouraging them to take responsibility or, even in areas where they cannot, by welcoming their advice and criticism, we can help to establish relationships based on human understanding and a common purpose, and they may learn the enormously important lesson that authority is there to be worked with and not against, that it is there to extend their *real* freedom (freedom *for* and not just freedom *from*), not simply to frustrate their every wish.

If the teenager's capacity for responsibility cannot be fully satisfied within the confines of home and school, no matter how much he takes over from his teachers the task of organizing duty groups, clubs, teams, external relations, then he must be introduced to the idea of service in a wider context. Not only home and school but also society must see that there are genuine opportunities for service available, well organized, with tangible results and with certainty of support, sympathy and recognition from the adult world. The very fact that some young people give boredom as an excuse for their antisocial behaviour should give us pause. It is not very helpful to say that we were never bored at their age and leave it at that. The young have an enormous reservoir of sheer physical energy and, although those who continually abuse our generation for the mess we have made of the world never give us credit for it, there has been no war to absorb that energy. They are also full of good-will and idealism, however incoherent and sometimes misdirected that may be. Here again, they lack a war.

This seems a terrible thing to say, and God forbid that war should come to redress the balance, but it seems to be a self-evident fact. This is the first generation that has grown to manhood and not been forced into uniform. Neither is it any use crying for a return to military service, for this is the last thing which will satisfy the restless energy of idealistic youth.

The violent opposition of so many young Americans to the war in Vietnam shows that the old appeals to patriotism will no longer inspire youth. Young men will not accept 'theirs not to reason why, theirs but to do or die', and a very good thing too. After all, not even the war against Nazi Germany was sufficient incentive to mobilize America, safe on the other side of the Atlantic, and it took the direct assault of the Japanese on Pearl Harbor to bring her into the war. Similarly, the British in 1939 were fighting not for Poland but for their own lives and freedom. It is not difficult to see why war in Vietnam fails completely to enlist the loyalty and enthusiasm of young Americans, and in fact intensifies their frustration. All the energy and idealism which in earlier times would have been directed into what they would have accepted as a 'just' war is bubbling and boiling over, and the only thing which their elders seem able to offer them is what to them is manifestly an 'unjust' war. Yet all the time they are looking for causes; and because our computerized society does not offer them genuine and varied organizing activities, genuine contributions to the community, regular service to the sick, the handicapped, the old, because they see no clear goal with a tangible result, the young go running wildly in all directions, like Don Quixote tilting at windmills and with as little result.

Has anyone noticed how quickly the enthusiasms of the young for their causes fade away? A few years ago everyone was banning the bomb and marching to Aldermaston; then for a few years it has been Vietnam which has occupied their minds, culminating in the great nationwide moratorium in America last year, with repercussions in other countries. Biological warfare has been a bit of a non-starter, although there have been a few half-hearted demos at Porton Down; and only a few cranks have taken up such lost causes as preaching pupil-power to schools and distributing birth-control literature to children. The great rallying-cry at the moment is apartheid, although in America, where it clearly has not the same appeal since the same links do not exist with South Africa, conservation is the 'in' thing and the young have all been earnestly marching and chanting in support of 'Earth Day'. Flower-power did not last

97

long in this country and red power has not yet got off the ground, one assumes because we have no Red Indians. Perhaps the British equivalent is Scottish and Welsh nationalism!

Much as one sympathizes with the idealism of the young, one does rather wish that there were less of an element of self-dramatization in their enthusiasms. How many of those who made such fools of themselves lying about Trafalgar Square on the tenth anniversary of the Sharpeville tragedy, pretending to be dead Africans, were old enough ten years ago to know what really happened, always providing that *anyone* knows what really happened? This sort of play-acting degrades the memory of the dead, and I find it infinitely more repellent than the harmless inanities of the *Black and White Minstrel Show* which gives such offence to some of the young. It was a similar kind of silly exhibitionism which led a number of young Americans solemnly to *bury* a brand-new car on 'Earth Day' as a protest against pollution. One would have been more impressed with their protest if they had not, immediately after, piled into cars and driven away!

What a pity it is that such futile antics are all that the young can find to satisfy their burning enthusiasm for a cause! Even though my own girls have raised a lot of money for *Shelter* by sponsored walks, I have the uneasy feeling that there is something slightly spurious about these activities and that it would be better if they could be occupied in something more positive and constructive than merely getting adults to pay them so much a mile for walking.

However, it does not help the young if we laugh at their rather self-righteous suffering, their bread-and-water lunches, their camping-out in simulated slums, their playing at war in Trafalgar Square, their occupying of property in the name of the homeless. It is up to us to ensure that their desire to be of service is properly harnessed, for service to others is one of the basic responsibilities which they should accept from as early an age as possible. The child who has always been accustomed to doing things for others, even little things like washing the dishes and cleaning the shoes, can very easily graduate to mowing the lawn for the old lady next door or running her errands, so that he grows up imbued with the spirit of ungrudging service. Never mind if he does not do these jobs as well as you could do them, even if he sometimes forgets to do them at all, it is still important to give him the opportunity. How much more vital it is that, when he is in his teens and early twenties, society should put his boundless enthusiasm and good-will to work, rather than let him spend himself in pointless demos, sit ins and protest marches, where he can be so easily moved to violence by any articulate misfit who is able to make absolute nonsense sound realistic and convincing.

I do not by any means claim to have thoroughly explored the whole subject of the rights and responsibilities of the young. Many of my readers will no doubt be able to think of other principles, of even greater priority than those which I have mentioned. There remains one more thing which we must at all costs try to teach the young, one more rule for living that we must ask them to accept, and that is respect for the personality of others. This is going to be of paramount importance when we look at what we are going to teach our children about their sexual relationships, but it is, of course, basic in all human and social contacts. It is not easy to turn the teenager's passionate preoccupation with his own uniqueness into an awareness and an admission that everyone else is equally unique and, therefore, has just as much right to consideration as he has; but we must try to do it.

We are always being told by the young that we do not understand them; but does it ever occur to them that they might occasionally make the effort to try to understand us? They are so proud of their good intentions and so convinced that, if only they could have their way, they would achieve heaven on earth, preferably by Monday morning. Do they never stop to think that we were once young and impatient, that we, when the time came, genuinely *tried* to right the wrongs which troubled our consciences, and that when they are our age another generation will reproach them for not caring and for having made a mess of things?

So much of their protest seems completely to ignore the genuine rights of other people, and all too often it is the rights of a minority which are being asserted at the expense of those of the majority. When a few militant students occupy university buildings, they probably think that they have a genuine grievance, although it seems as though their preoccupation with such issues as political files, representation on committees, etcetera, is more means to an end than an end in itself. But in ventilating the grievance of a few, they are disrupting the studies, wasting the time and often bringing into disrepute the reputation of the many.

Again, much as I deplore the whole sorry business of apartheid, and though I personally would probably not have voted for the white South African teams to be invited to this country, I *can* see the other side. It may be that the best way to influence opinion in South Africa, at least in the direction of multiracial sport, is to invite more rather than fewer teams, and make sure that they play against as many non-white people as possible. But quite apart from this consideration, which Peter Hain and his fanatical young followers simply will not listen to, I do not believe that I have the right to tell rugby and cricket clubs whom they must or must not play against, and I certainly have not the right to tell members of the public whom they must watch playing. Whether we like it or not, the majority of the population of this country probably *did* want to watch the Springboks, and it seems to me quite monstrous that they should have been prevented from so doing because of the conscience of a minority. I am sure that the demonstrators feel absolutely splendid—knights in shining armour—now they have stopped a cricket tour and struck a blow for the poor down-trodden Africans, but, actually, all they have done is to satisfy their own egos at the expense of the rights of the majority. And they have done precisely nothing for the Africans. In short, under cover of a selfless altruism, they have acted with a total disregard for anyone but themselves.

This self-regard, this arrogant assertion that no one has any right to an opinion except yourself, is exhibited in the deplorable scenes at universities and elsewhere when speakers, whose political views happen not to suit the demonstrators, have been invited to appear, often to speak on quite non-political matters.

They are shouted down, sometimes physically assaulted: whatever may be the views for and against, it is inexcusable that Enoch Powell, the American Ambassador, the Foreign Secretary, the Home Secretary, Denis Healey, Dr Inch of the Biological Research Station at Porton, Patrick Wall, M.P., and his wife, should all be mobbed and threatened by hostile students when other students, certainly a majority, had invited them to the universities concerned. It is, after all, the criminal mentality which allows a person to behave in complete disregard of anyone's feelings and rights but his own, that will permit even the killing of anyone who stands in his way and thwarts his desires. We have all seen very small children work themselves up to a screaming rage when inanimate objects have resisted their efforts to move them, but they are too young to know what they are doing. When young men—and intelligent young men at that—behave in this dangerously infantile way, something has clearly been missing from their upbringing and they have grown to manhood totally devoid of any consciousness of the rights of a person other than themselves.

The comment of the Vice-Chancellor of Oxford on the students who invaded his garden armed with trumpets, tambourines and dustbin lids, banging on his windows and beating on his doors, and who continued to do so even when they realized that he was out and after they had been courteously invited in to talk to his wife, was that they reminded him of his two-year-old grandson. They did not, they said, recognize private property, and they interspersed their banging and blowing with a ritual incantation of obscenities which seems to be a compulsive act by the female demonstrator, apparently anxious to prove that she is as free and fearless as her male counterpart. Can anything at all have been done during the childhood and adolescence of these mindless young people to teach them respect for the personality of others?

Not, be it noted, respect for authority nor for one's elders and betters nor for any of the other idols which were set up for earlier generations to worship and which the young of today have, in most cases quite rightly, rejected, but simply a *readiness*—no more than that—to respect the essential and inviolate uniqueness of every human being and his right to preserve it and not join the herd, either from fear or any other unworthy motive, for anything which threatens the freedom and integrity of the individual threatens the whole foundation of our civilization.

8

The Sexploited Generation

This matter of respect for the personality of others and the right of other people to preserve their integrity is fundamental to what we should be teaching our children about sexual morality.

There is probably no area of modern permissiveness which generates more heat and less light than this: witness the passions raised in Parliament and elsewhere over the Bills concerned with homosexuality, abortion and divorce, and the quite extraordinary storm in a teacup over the move to allow the Secretary of State for Education to supplement grants for students cohabiting with a member of the opposite sex. Incidentally, why only a member of the *opposite* sex? One gathers that this financial provision through grants for the dependent partner in an unmarried ménage is not to be absolutely confined to cases where there are children involved. If one is to take this to its logical conclusion, is there any reason for not giving a supplementary grant to a student who supports a partner of the *same* sex, providing that partnership is seen to be stable and lasting? Homosexual behaviour between consenting adults in private has, quite rightly and not before time, ceased to be a criminal offence. If we are to go along with Lord Beaumont of Whitley in thinking that the State has no right to discriminate between people on the basis of their private morals, I cannot see that it should be prepared not only to condone but also to subsidize, through the tax-payer, illicit heterosexual unions while discriminating against homosexual ones. Let me hasten to add, before anyone protests that this would be permissiveness gone mad, that of course it would, but it still seems to me the logical development of some of the 'liberal' thinking of the supporters of the Education (Miscellaneous Provisions) Bill.

The Lord Chancellor said that it was 'almost unheard of' for a grant to be made where there were no children. In this context *almost* is not good enough. Widows and unmarried

THE VULNERABLE GENERATION

women who somehow manage to live (and even to remain reasonably sane and cheerful) without the support, either financial or psychological, of a lover, have every reason to object to any portion of the tax which they pay going to provide undergraduates with what used to be known—quite inaccurately, since everything has to be paid for by someone in one way or another—as free love. In this case it would seem to be the tax-payer who foots the bill.

I suppose that before I say anything more on this whole vexed question of sexual *mores*, I should make my own position clear. I happen to believe that chastity before marriage and fidelity within it are not obsolete but are abiding requisites of respect for the whole personality. I also believe that if it were possible to ask the population of these islands, men, women and children over the age of twelve, whether or not they agreed with me, a large majority would answer 'yes'. I know that there is absolutely no way of proving such an assumption and that I shall be greeted with derisive laughter in certain quarters for making it, but I shall continue to maintain that it is true. I *know* that the statistics can be depressing. We are told of the rise in the number of divorces. We know that many children are born considerably less than nine months after their parents' marriage and that, until abortion became legal, the number of illegitimate births had continued to rise steeply. The fact that these unwanted pregnancies are now terminated does not seem to me to be as much a matter for congratulation as some of our social reformers seem to think. We hear that even the Home Secretary is not too happy that London has become known as the abortion capital of the world. Neither can the Minister of Health be very pleased that the V.D. clinics recorded 44,962 new cases of gonorrhoea in 1968—an increase of eighty-two per cent over the total for 1957.

The danger is that, confronted with these admittedly unpleasant facts, we may be shocked into ignoring the other side of the coin. Whatever the divorce rate, the very great majority of married people stay married until death them do part and do not ever even seriously contemplate anything else. I am reminded of the story of the couple celebrating their Diamond

Wedding who were asked if they had never once thought of divorce. After some reflection it was the wife who answered, 'Divorce? Never! *Murder* frequently, but never *divorce*!'

I forget what the actual percentage is of first-born children who have provably been conceived outside marriage, but it is certainly small in comparison with the number of those who respectably arrive after the requisite nine months are up. Though one cannot exactly rejoice at 20,000 abortions, the fact still remains that the overwhelming majority of women have never had one and have no intention of ever having one. Nearly 45,000 new cases of venereal disease in one year is disturbing, but it is still true that most people in this country are as unlikely to catch V.D. as they are to catch leprosy. And after all the fuss about providing grants for students' mistresses, we learn that only about ten people are involved at any one time. Whether it is indeed worth spending so much of Parliament's time for the the sake of ten young people apparently unable or unwilling to exercise self-control until they can afford to support a wife and family is perhaps debatable, but the picture which has been painted of the universities positively wallowing in sexual promiscuity is really rather overdone.

Yet having said all that, one is still left with the inescapable conclusion that the world today is far too concerned with sex, and that many influences are at work, in art and literature, in television, film and theatre, in the mass media of communication and even in advertising—indeed, especially in advertising— which are having the net result of cheapening and trivializing the sexual relationship. It is constantly kept before the eyes and in the mind of the young who are at an age when sexual feelings are very easily aroused and only with difficulty controlled. If we look back for a moment to Our Man from the Thirties, suddenly awaking to the full impact of the Seventies, he might be forgiven for imagining that this so-called civilized society had only just discovered sex.

We are told of the prurience of the Victorians in covering up the legs of their pianos—incidentally, is this really true? Has anyone any actual proof that the Victorians did this? My grandparents were, I suppose, Victorians, but a livelier quartet of thoroughly forward-looking people I have never met. But even if they did, I cannot see that this indicates a less healthy state of mind than that of so many people today who are virtually obsessed with sex, for they think, talk, write, paint nothing else. If we are not very careful, sex will be in grave danger of becoming one big bore, the non-event of the Seventies, an obligation rather than a joy.

It has already suffered the fate of being the 'in' thing: there are certain films one must see, books one must read, plays and art exhibitions one must attend, however excruciatingly bad and boring one secretly finds them, because they either have been banned or else are advertised as 'the film [book, play, exhibition, etcetera] which they said we did not *dare* produce'. Middle-aged critics write cautious praise of a play which exploits every aspect of sex and in which every other word is an obscenity, because they apparently dare not admit, for fear of being labelled square, that they found the whole thing revolting and a bore into the bargain. If John Lennon's lithographs had been on anything else but sexual themes, no doubt someone would have had the honesty to say that they were not very good; but because he is a pop star who has made himself and his wife notorious by their antics in bed in Amsterdam and elsewhere, we are asked to accept these childish graffiti as serious art, instead of the sort of thing more usually seen on the walls of the less salubrious public lavatories. I yield to no one in my sincere admiration of the gigantic genius of Picasso, but I cannot believe that the senile eroticism of his latest engravings has either enhanced his reputation or enriched our artistic experience.

And what is one to think of this quotation from the *Sunday Times*? 'Bob Godfrey is 48 and he's been making cartoon films all his life for fun. Now he thinks he's made one which will make a spot of money, thanks to the X certificate he's won from the film censor.' According to the report, he apparently discussed with the censor beforehand what he would have to put in the film in order to qualify for the coveted X. *The Times* showed one shot from the cartoon of a man exposing himself to two elderly women in a park. Are we supposed to find this amusing? I once taught in a school next to a public park and it was a not uncommon occurrence for terrified children to run into school in the morning after just such an experience. I should like to assure Mr Godfrey and John Trevelyan, the film censor, that it is not as hilarious as all that.

I have already made my point about the totally unnecessary introduction of sexual encounters into so many television plays and the dreary repetitiousness of so much fiction. It is all so predictable and, it seems to me, such a very easy way of filling up the printed page. Anyone with the smallest talent for writing and, I maintain, with or without actual sexual experience, could turn out this sort of blow-by-blow account by the chapterful. After all, if we are going to be frank about sex, let us admit once and for all that one orgasm is very like another and leave it at that. What on earth is the point of reading, in every novel we pick up, the same old descriptions of the same old act? Even if our daring young author *has* just discovered it and is just longing to write down all those lovely four-letter words, there is nothing new to be said about the sex act, which must surely be just about the most old-fashioned thing there is. After yet another basinful of stark realism, I find myself longing for some nice suggestive asterisks! In fact, I often think that many of the love scenes in modern novels are enough to put the uninitiated off sex for life.

Sex has become a sort of exhibitionism, with everyone trying to outdo everyone else in inventiveness. Even the literary critics have got in on the act. I recall one review of Adam Diment's first novel in which his 'hero' waxed lyrical about the joys of intercourse after smoking pot, as dangerous a piece of writing to put in the hands of an adolescent as I have ever read. One reviewer commented knowingly that the author had somewhat exaggerated the aphrodisiac effects of marijuana. The inference was obvious: he wanted us to know that he too had had sex after smoking pot. To which one feels inclined to retort, 'So what?' I am no more interested in the sex life of the literary critic of my Sunday paper than I am in that of the schoolboy who delivers it.

For the average person who does not find it either instructive or entertaining eternally to think about sex, modern living sometimes presents a bleak prospect. Finding himself with a free evening, he picks up his newspaper and looks for a film. If he had happened to live in my part of the world last week he would not have found one cinema showing a film without an X certificate. So he decides to stay at home and read his library book. Soon bored with its turgid psychological introversion and its boring descriptions of intercourse, 'normal', oral and anal, as in one well-reviewed novel by an author of repute which I happened to read recently, he switches on the television, only to be confronted with one of the B.B.C.'s adventures in modern drama. In desperation he decides to turn off the features and only watch the commercials, but even here sex raises its draggy old head. For, according to the *Times* reporters, 'probably the most purposefully titillating scene of the week occurred in a commercial for cigars in which a girl on a beach at first appeared topless, and was seen later emerging from the sea clutching her breasts which were apparently covered only by a thin, wet shirt'.

If our fugitive from sexual allusion and innuendo should then turn to his newspapers, what does he find? That sex has obviously become a very good selling-line with the advertisers, many of whom seem to think it obligatory to market their wares, from cigarettes to cars, with the aid of naked or half-naked girls either alone or in clinches with similarly attired men. The sexy innuendo, evoking the sly snigger, and the double-entendre with a sexual connotation are now part of the stock-in-trade of advertising. Here are some examples of the sort of thing to which I am referring and which, I think, could well be omitted from our newspapers and periodicals without much loss to the advertisers and with a certain amount of advantage to the general moral climate in which the young are growing up.

A recent Sunday colour supplement carried in the same edition advertisements for women's underclothing and men's sportswear. Five full pages were entirely devoted to colour photographs which would not have been out of place in a collection of erotica. The underclothing was displayed in the fashionable legs-wide-apart stance so that the first part of the anatomy which hits the eye as one turns the page is the crotch, subtly shaded so as to suggest the pubic hair under the fabric of the minuscule pants, just as the nipples are prominently displayed under the bra. The accompanying blurb referred to 'free-thinking designers'! The sports clothes were advertised in fifteen colour photographs, of which fourteen showed a couple in varying stages of semi-nudity and intimate embrace, in the sea, in a field, on the beach. Quite apart from the usual generous display of thighs and navels, several of the women's garments would almost certainly have been banned on any British beach and a good number of Continental ones, for they were so constructed that the slightest puff of wind or even a movement from the wearer would leave the breasts entirely bare. In order to sell a man's white towelling jacket, it was apparently thought essential to show him with his open mouth clamped on a girl's, whose almost naked breasts were pressed against him and whose naked thighs were wrapped around one of his Bermuda-shorted legs. In fact, the impression left by this particular advertisement was not of men's clothes but of women's lack of them, and one really had to read the accompanying script in order to find out what was actually being offered for sale.

A few months ago a highly reputable and respectable car was advertised with the slogan: *Miss So-and-So got a lot of experience in the back of this car*, accompanied by a picture of a rather prim, getting-on-for-middle-aged woman simpering coyly on the back seat. Of course, the admen are going to insist virtuously that it is all in the mind and that if I see sexual innuendo in that, I must have a dirty mind. The advertisement clearly stated that Miss Whatsit got *secretarial* experience. What ever else did I think it meant? Of course, they know quite well what I think it meant, which is what everyone else who saw the advertisement thought it meant and what in fact we were intended to think.

Now, I do not want to make too much of this growing tendency to use nudity, with or without sexual undertones, and this rather juvenile sexual jokiness for advertisement purposes, otherwise I shall be accused of being obsessed myself, and I know all too well that an unmarried woman is always fair game for that kind of stupid and cruel jibe. No one in his right mind is going to suggest that our young people are being whipped up into sexual frenzy by being constantly exposed to advertisements where the emphasis is on the sexual characteristics of a woman's body, but I do think that there are dangers. In the first place, this sort of thing is almost certainly stimulating to adolescents, who have a difficult enough time as it is without being constantly reminded of a woman's physical attractions. Next, in a world where women are at last achieving some sort of status and escaping from the traditional role of second-class citizen, is it valid to reduce them in the adman's fantasy to nothing more than sexual objects?

Again, even in this wonderful free and uninhibited world, I still have a sneaking feeling that sexual love is something which a couple should want to keep to themselves and not parade before an audience. Exhibitionism is not an especially normal trait, and I confess to preferring the convention which reserves the more intimate embraces of lovers for the times when they are alone. The day may indeed come when people will not be at all embarrassed at picking their way over the bodies of naked, embracing couples in the park or on the beach, and no doubt there are some who would argue that the sooner it comes the better. I do not happen to think so, and I deplore this present trend which gives the impression that it is a normal and natural thing for physical love-making to be carried on in public. *It is not*; and I think that the intimate lives of all lovers will be immeasurably impoverished if it should ever become so. A man and woman in love are surely something more than copulating animals, and human society should not be reduced to the level of a farmyard.

But I think that my main objection to the constant parade of sex which seems to fill so much of modern life is that, while filling the eyes and the minds of the young until it risks becoming an unhealthy and dangerous obsession, at the same time it manages to make trivial and of no significance something which surely must be one of the more important human activities. Maybe there is something to be said for the school of thought which would assert that we have made too much of a mystery of sex in the past, and that it is a sign of mental health to tear off the trappings of romance and reticence which are really symbols of fear and prudery, but I shall be very sorry to see a world where the sexual relationship becomes just another appetite like eating or drinking, a world 'liberated' by birth-control and abortion and where promiscuity is the norm. It was, I think, Friedrich Engels who said that sex should be as natural as a drink of water. How many earnest young Marxists have attempted the virginity of their girl-friends with that phrase? It was tried on me once, and I can still see the utter astonishment on the face of my would-be lover when I answered him with the rest of the quotation, conveniently ignored by those who would cite Communist scripture to their purpose: 'But who wants to drink from a glass greasy from the lips of others?'

Cannot therefore the adult world get over its hang-up on sex and give the young a chance to get back to good, old-fashioned romance? By which I do not mean Ethel M. Dell and E. M. Hull, nor even Barbara Cartland, but the Keatsean 'huge cloudy symbols of a high romance' which surely should loom through the imagination of our boys and girls. Because they have an enormous appetite for it, as witness the quite extraordinary songs which will suddenly shoot to the top of the charts against all the predictions of the purists. Christmas or no, whoever could have foreseen the fantastic success of 'Two Little Boys'? Neither is it only the Mums and Dads who buy the schmaltzy ballads of Ken Dodd and Andy Williams, or the simple sentimentality of Val Doonican. I have found it touching and significant to see, in the middle of the frenzied jungle beat of *Top of the Pops*, the young suddenly still and dreaming to the quiet tenderness of Simon and Garfunkel's 'Bridge Over Troubled Water'. Let us for goodness' sake—and I use the word advisedly—rescue sex both from the gutter of commercial exploitation through which it has been dragged and from the plane of exhibitionism, even status-symbol, where it now sometimes rests.

In the teenage world where to conform is everything, the danger of the status-symbol approach to sex is obvious. Most of us will remember how the adult world was rocked by the 'golliwog girls', who wore yellow golliwogs as a sign that they had lost their virginity, and it is not so very long since a reporter from the *Times Educational Supplement* visited an Essex college of further education and found that the sixteen-year-olds were competing to see who could lose her virginity the first. I am willing to bet that some if not most of those golliwogs reposed on blameless bosoms. The silly children were ashamed to admit that they were still chaste, because they thought that it was abnormal to be so. I have read a letter written by a fourteen-year-old in which she claimed to be having a torrid affair with the boy next door, all for the benefit of the friend to whom she was writing, who had indeed had sexual experience and had boasted of it. The pressures of group opinion are never more dangerous than in this context, and it is surely deplorable that, instead of doing everything to help the young to withstand these pressures, the adult world makes it more and more easy for them to succumb.

I suppose because I am a woman and because my life has been devoted to the education of girls, I am bound to look at sexual questions from a woman's point of view. I have never considered myself a feminist and can truthfully say with the song-writer, 'I enjoy being a girl.' Even though I am an only child and was brought up along with two boy cousins and their friends, I never remember having the slightest desire to be a boy and I view the world of unisex with considerable distaste. I can imagine nothing more dreary than the fate of women in a recent television documentary where militant and aggressive feminists advocated the sort of world in which there was absolutely no difference between the male and female roles.

I am delighted that women are slowly being released from the bondage of past centuries, for Heaven knows they have paid over and over again for the sins of Eve. The history of women is a story of cruelty and oppression beside which the slave trade pales into insignificance, and they have still a long way to go before they reach full stature in a world which will remain for the foreseeable future a man's world. Beyond any doubt, the new sexual freedom of women is an important step in the right direction and the contraceptive pill makes it possible, for virtually the first time in the history of the world, for a woman to call her body her own. Or does it? If the present trend continues and intensifies, shall we not find that women are now slaves to a far worse tyranny, and one moreover which gives far greater advantages to the male sex than ever the old one did?

In the 'bad old days' it was assumed that a girl was chaste until she married. Most normal young men did their best to alter this state of affairs, but without a great deal of hope of success. If they succeeded, no doubt they were delighted, but if they did not—and usually they did not—they neither bullied nor complained but accepted their rebuff with resignation. What is more, the vast majority seemed to thrive on this self-denial, and I would be surprised if statistics could prove that there were fewer happy marriages then than now, or more neurotic women ending up in mental hospitals. What is to be the assumption in the brave new world of unisex? That every man has a right to any woman whom he fancies since she is liberated from the fear of consequences? Young women of my acquaintance have complained bitterly to me that this already seems to be assumed by some young men. If a girl does not immediately respond to an invitation to go to bed, she runs the risk of being asked if she is lesbian. I can see no advantage whatsoever for a girl to be freed from the necessity of chastity only to be subjected to the necessity of promiscuity, and in fact I should think that the average girl would much prefer the former state.

It is easy to see why men, being on the whole polygamous animals and very much quicker on the trigger sexually than women, should view with joyful anticipation a world where every girl is there for the asking, with no embarrassing consequences in the shape of an unwanted baby and therefore no danger of actually having to marry the girl. But is this such a rosy future for women? Is this what they want? Because if they are not extremely careful, this is what they are going to get. Girls are being asked, in the sacred name of sexual freedom, to violate their most precious and innate instincts.

I do not care a button for what the psychiatrists say—most of them male, anyway, and so used to dealing with abnormality that they cannot recognize the normal when they see it. This book is not written for them nor with their patients in mind. I am talking about the teenage daughters of the average ordinary woman in the street. These girls are not nymphomaniacs: they have the normal physical desires of the adolescent but they also have the normal built-in physical and mental safeguards of any girl of that age, among which I would rank first an innate sense of modesty. The conquest of that modesty by her husband should be a joyous experience for both of them. What possible satisfaction does any man get, other than the purely physical release of orgasm, in the conquest of a woman whose defences go down for any man? And what woman can feel complimented by the attentions of a man who lays siege to every woman he meets?

I can visualize nothing so utterly boring and insipid as a state of affairs where everyone has access to everyone else on demand. I think it was the hero of *The Dolly, Dolly Spy* who, on contemplating an evening out which would inevitably end in bed, thought wryly that he almost believed the old arrangements were better—then you could not expect to sleep with any girl, now you had to sleep with everybody. An obligation rather than a joy. How sad!

Girls have everything to lose and precious little to gain by lightly surrendering their virginity. Times may have changed since Byron wrote that 'man's love is of man's life a thing apart,/ 'Tis woman's whole existence', but there is still an element of truth in this complacent statement. When a woman begins to be interested in a man, her first and automatic thought is not whether he is likely to be good in bed; the silly creature sees herself first showing off an engagement ring and then in white satin and orange-blossom floating down the aisle to the strains of *Lohengrin*.

I am sorry if this outrages the ardent feminists and disappoints the men who, judging by the sort of female portrayed by most male novelists, live in a romantic dream of women who are driven mad with lust by every man they see. But women on the whole are rather simple souls with some quite basic desires for a husband, a home and children. If I dare whisper it, with quite a number of women, the first of these three is often a means to an end—the other two. What they do *not* want is a series of mad, passionate, sexy affairs. Mrs Patrick Campbell spoke from the bottom of every woman's heart when she spoke of the deep peace of the marriage bed after the hurly-burly of the chaise-longue.

I cannot imagine that the average man, after he has had intercourse, begins to wonder whether he has begotten a child. It is one of the crazy biological facts of life that a woman, when she lies with a man, wants a child. This may sound utter nonsense in the face of those 20,000 abortions, but my women readers will know what I am talking about. Poor lunatic creatures that we are, with our bodies geared to the rhythms of the moon and tides, we go around wondering why we are feeling depressed until we remember that we are due to menstruate and that our empty wombs are lamenting another wasted month and no child conceived. This is true of any woman, be she wife, mistress or virgin, and however much she may frustrate the purposes of her body, either by chastity or by birth-control.

I knew a woman who married so late in life that neither she nor her husband imagined that they wanted to start a family. When she thought that she was pregnant she was utterly dismayed and fervently hoped to be mistaken. She was—and wept bitterly when she found it so. The tragic case reported of a woman who, after eight years of marriage, found the thought of her life being interrupted by a first baby too much for her, had an abortion and then was so overcome with guilt and depression that she took her own life at the age of thirty-three, does not surprise me at all. The surprising thing is that there have not been more such cases.

I spoke of the violation of woman's deepest instincts when the permissive society demands that she make herself available, like the temple prostitutes in the olden days, to all comers. The necessary developments of this promiscuity further outrage her essential womanhood, by requiring her ceaselessly to prevent the conception of life or, the ultimate degradation, to destroy the life within her. If this is the price woman has to pay for freedom, then give me tyranny any day.

I have deliberately not spoken about morals. I happen to

think that it *is* morally wrong to use someone purely as an instrument of physical pleasure and that fear of consequences is no basis for self-control. Respect for another person's integrity, both physical and spiritual, insists on self-restraint, and love demands the kind of self-giving which is also self-denying. If we can succeed in teaching this to our children, we,—and what is more important, *they*—will be saved a lot of heartache. But even if the moral approach fails—though I see no reason why it should in the setting of the stable, happy family life that I have postulated as essential for a child's well-being—then it may well be that they will appreciate some of my more materialistic arguments listed above. If the boys do not and the girls do, then we shall simply be back at square one, with not very hopeful young men attempting the chastity of not very impressionable young women; and how restful it will be for all concerned!

So high on the list of subjects on which I should like to declare a moratorium is sex. Let us, young and old alike, make an effort to get it back in its proper place. Let us stop prostituting it in cheap commercials, in films, books, plays, exhibitions which would never come before the public eye at all were it not for 'sexploitation'—we even have a word for it now. Let the designers tear up their vulgar topless dresses and see-through blouses, and give our young women clothes which do not make them look like tarts. Let us stop calling obscenity 'fearless realism' and promiscuity 'a creative relationship'. Above all let us teach our children to distinguish between the primitive reaction to desire—'I want therefore I grab'—and the truly civilized 'I want, but if it is best, I can wait or I can even say no'.

9

Honest to God ?

In any discussion of what we should be teaching our children it is impossible to ignore the thorny question of religious instruction.

The point has already been made that much of the bewilderment of the young and the uncertainty of their elders stems directly from a decline in religious belief. Those ardent crusaders for secularism who never miss an opportunity to jeer at the deluded fools who still believe in a god have much to answer for. However sincerely held their beliefs or even valid their criticisms of organized religion, they have done almost irreparable damage by their reckless undermining of the faith which, with all its faults and weaknesses, has at least upheld moral standards and given some degree of strength and comfort to humanity for many generations. They have knocked away the props and put nothing in their place.

I once heard Professor C. A. Coulson, the eminent mathematician and Fellow of the Royal Society say, 'The old phrase *sub specie aeternitatis*, under the gaze of eternity, is a phrase that has rather dropped out of the thinking of today, and yet, unless we can bring it in, and as we bring it in not in any sense slow down this great movement of change and progress, I believe there will be no ultimate health in our community.' I personally find within the Christian religion, if it is properly understood (and I find it nowhere else), a big enough outlook to cope with the problems of the 1970s. To quote yet again from Professor Coulson: 'Power without purpose, freedom without responsibility, science without conscience, cannot ever be a fulfilment of mankind . . . the purpose, the responsibility, and the conscience are going to be found in that sense of eternity. . . . The kind of life which quite obviously can be for the fulfilling and the enriching of everyone alive will be so because there will be those who . . . have recognized that the passing circumstances of life, however rapidly they move, can always be an expression of that which lies beyond and behind them all, the spirit and the will of God.'

The Christian believes that morals are not merely a matter of human relationships but that they affect man's relationship to God and that it *is* possible to define what is right and good. There are those who will tell us that we have no authority to teach a particular philosophy of life, for how can we know that we are right? Are we then to be so afraid of doing the wrong thing that we do nothing at all? By all means, let the young be made aware of the variety of ethical codes existing in the world for, as the late Archbishop Temple said in his book *Christian Faith and Life*, 'The variety of ethical codes in different parts of the world presupposes agreement in one thing, that there is a difference between right and wrong.' Young people must be able to choose for themselves but they must have something to choose from. They must learn from committed adults a philosophy of life that works, for they will not find it among their own age-group.

To those who are committed Christians, Christianity seems the most humane of religions, and the message of Christ and His Spirit are the things that they live by. They are unceasingly aware of the immense debt owed by humanity to that Spirit. How are they to set about sharing that conviction with the young, in the face of the opposition and derision of the secularists? Much that I have already said about the values which we should be teaching applies specifically to Christ and to all He stands for: the value of persons who should never be used merely for our pleasure or profit; the value of work as a thing to be enjoyed and to take a pride in; the value of matching freedom with discipline.

No one will pretend that it is easy to be a Christian: that is why we must offer to our children the help that they will need if they are going to succeed in living by Christian principles. How can we bring a child to see Christian worship as an essential part of his life? Pressures are intensifying in all quarters to abolish the daily assembly in schools and the weekly lesson of religious instruction. I believe that we must rethink both our religious instruction and its practice, but that to abolish them altogether is to knock out yet one more prop from under the already tottering young.

It is an interesting thing that in America, where religious teaching has long been forbidden in the schools, there is a tremendous demand, especially by the young, for what has been described as 'offbeat religion and the occult'. Several high schools and at least three universities are giving courses in witchcraft, one of which, at the University of New York, is being run by a self-styled witch who maintains that there are four hundred covens in the United States and sees in this evidence of a great religious revival among the young. If this is true, what an indictment of our teaching! The children ask for a fish and we give them a serpent, they seek a god and we offer them the Devil.

The drug-cult of such people as Timothy Leary, the pop preoccupation with Hindu ritual and the phony teachings of so-called swamis, even the hippie cult, are all replacements for Christianity, eagerly turned to by those young people who have been alienated from the old beliefs and left without any apparent purpose in life. They find that they still need a reason for living, an answer to the eternal questions: why am I here and where am I going? All the young are looking for something but what help are they getting in their search?

It is the positive duty of those who profess and call themselves Christians (and a majority still do even though our churches are empty), not to *send* their children to church but to take them. Most of those who complain that church services are dreary and utterly out of touch with the realities of life have probably never been inside their parish church or any other for years, so how can they know? One of the encouraging things on T.V. is the weekly *Songs of Praise*. Of course, it is easy to be cynical and say that the church is only packed because it is on television, but even the most hard-boiled cynic must sometimes find the innocent faces of the very young, and even the occasional self-conscious smiles, hastily concealed, of the teenagers when they realize that the camera is trained upon them, rather touching. I frankly do not believe that all these young people have suddenly rushed to church and learned a few hymns, simply so that they can be 'on the telly'. I think that they have found what they were seeking in their church, which is not just a place reserved for baptisms and weddings, but one whose influence penetrates right into the stuff of their everyday life.

Sometimes it is easy to see why the churches are empty. No one wants to go there to listen to erudite sermons on abstruse texts, but there are few priests nowadays who preach in this sterile fashion. It is the wholeness of the Christian faith with which they concern themselves and its relevance to life in the modern world. If only parents would *go* to their church instead of sitting at home on Sunday tut-tutting over the latest teenage scandal and asking indignantly what the Church is doing about it—for, after all, what *is* the Church? It is the *ecclesia*—the assembly of the people, not the bishops and clergy, the College of Cardinals or the Vatican Council. At least, that is what it should be, what it was in the time of the apostles, and if the leaders of the church have made it into something different they must look to their consciences and see where they have gone wrong. A church which in the Seventies still forbids birth control, insists on the celibacy of its clergy and makes extraordinary gestures like the proposed canonization of the English martyrs is not likely to say very much to young people looking for spiritual guidance in an overpopulated world where sexual satisfaction is represented to them as of paramount importance, and where the bestial cruelty of man to man outdoes anything ever devised by those who burned the martyrs, whether Protestant or Catholic.

Nor is the Anglican Church in any better array. Many of its bishops are so busy sitting on the fence when moral questions are put to them that they begin to resemble the classic definition of a mugwump—an animal with its mug on one side of the fence and its wump on the other. Can we really ask the young to take seriously a church which holds a service to bless silkworms (presumably before slaughtering them in their thousands for their silk)? Or a bishop who actually suggests that opponents of the South African Test matches should pray for rain? A fitting comment on this piece of fatuous advice was given in *The Times* by another Anglican who thought the calling-down of fire and brimstone might be more effective, or the making of little wax images of the touring team and sticking pins in them the night before each Test match was due to start. The undignified spectacle of eminent churchmen sitting, marching, waving placards in defence of this, that or the other fashionably progressive cause does them and the Church which they represent no good at all. The militant young are not impressed for they sense their insincerity, and the non-militant lose whatever respect they may have had for them.

Nevertheless, despite all the weaknesses and shortcomings of some churchmen, there are still, in all parts of our land, parish churches and chapels which are centres of a true and living faith. If only more, not only of the young but also of their elders, would return to the habits of their childhood, they might get a pleasant surprise and discover that Christ still has meaning for them. In common with every other thinking person, I have known a period when I drifted away from church-going, and it is only over the last few years that I have come to know again the sanctifying and sustaining effect of worshipping together.

I know that in many schools today, particularly in the boarding schools, there is said to be a revolt against the daily service. This is the very excuse which the secularists are looking for in their campaign to prohibit compulsory religion in schools. If no effort is spared to make our religious teaching clear, positive and progressive, with plenty of discussion against a background of factual knowledge, the young will be ready to listen. Similarly, if they can be drawn into the services and made to feel that the real business of religion is life, they will not rebel against attending them.

Some of the most impressive services that we have held in our school chapel have been not the great choral occasions such as Confirmation or the service for leavers but the times when a particular form has selected a theme and composed a whole service, prayers, reading and music around it. I remember the first such service when some of our parents were present. They said to me afterwards in astonishment that they had no idea that their daughters felt so deeply about their faith and its relevance to the world's problems.

Another time, because all the seniors intended spending the entire Saturday on a sponsored walk for *Shelter*, the chaplain decided not to celebrate Holy Communion at seven the next morning and so give them the unaccustomed luxury of a long lie-in. To his utter astonishment, a deputation came and asked for a Celebration on the Saturday, before they set off for the walk. They came to the Communion table in slacks, boots and anoraks, ready for off, and dedicated to God the task which they had set themselves. This was a purely voluntary service and every confirmed member of the school attended. We make a great mistake if we assume that, because the vociferous doubters and rebels shout that they want no part of organized Christianity, they represent the whole of their age-group. We must beware lest we communicate our own adult doubts to children who are still prepared to accept the simple faith of childhood.

I know that many boys and girls in their middle years, perhaps at the sixth-form stage, will fall away from this faith. I have distinct recollections of the long discussions of my sixth-form days, where all or most of us firmly declared our atheism or at least agnosticism. Indeed, I remember taking rather a pride in loftily announcing that I was an agnostic when most of the form plumped for atheism. I felt it was more truly intellectual to say that one did not know! But if the faith has ever been there, if the hymns and prayers and rituals are part of the furniture of the mind, how easy it is to return in later years, when more experience of life and maturer judgement bring us to the realization that the crux of the issues which concern man ultimately lies in the spiritual aspect of human nature.

> There was a young girl from a mission
> Who was seized with an awful suspicion
> That original sin
> Didn't matter a pin
> In the era of nuclear fission.

So runs the limerick, but whatever our attitude to sin, original or otherwise, we all have to discover for ourselves what it means to be human, we have to concern ourselves with the ultimate nature of man, and here Christ will always have something valid to say to us.

I know that there is strong opposition to 'processing' a whole age-group through Confirmation, as I believe may still happen in some public schools—though not, I hasten to add, in any known to me, and certainly not in my own. Nevertheless, I would deplore any suggestion that children who are old enough to understand what they are being asked to do should not be actively encouraged to be confirmed, and so become full members of their church. I can easily imagine a situation where a boy, for instance, having been confirmed, later falls away from regular worship. Should he then meet a girl and marry her and she, a practising Christian, goes regularly to church with their children, how easy it will be for him to slip back into the old habits. If he has never had the habit, it will be much more difficult and one will see mother and children going off to church while father washes the car, goes to the pub or watches T.V., raising the obvious question in the children's minds.

We have come a long way from the days when children did what was right because God said so, but I still believe that, deep inside every human being, there is some kind of intuition of right. What is more, most children have a basic wish to do right, or at any rate to be thought by their elders to be doing right! Here again, I am not talking of the mentally disturbed or the downright delinquent for I have no relevant experience on which to draw and I do not therefore presume to make any suggestions as to how they should be handled. I am concerned solely with the average child and he, on the whole, likes to be liked and approved of. One of the roles of religion, to put it no higher, can surely be to reinforce the child's own innate feeling for what is praiseworthy.

With older children, the schools can help very considerably by making certain that they are fully aware of the truly Christian attitude to the matters which concern them passionately. I do not mean orthodox views of any particular church, for here we obviously come up against a difficulty. What, for instance, can we say is the 'Christian' attitude to birth-control if by 'Christian' we mean what is taught in the churches? What I mean is this: we should give every encouragement to the young to discuss colour prejudice, illegitimacy, the Pill, drugs, the bomb, pacifism, capital punishment, strikes—all the burning questions of the day—and in our discussions we should let them see, without dogmatizing or insisting that they think the same way, what we as committed Christians believe. We should encourage them to explore the teaching of Jesus for themselves and find out what His attitude would be to the things which so concern them, and so lead them to a realization that Christianity is not just an ancient creed or even an inspired story about a brave and good man. It is the key to victorious living, a faith for today.

Let us counter the parrot-cry of religion being the opiate of the people by showing the young what Christian Aid is doing for the world's poor and underprivileged, and that it was Jesus who first taught men to love not only their neighbours but their enemies. It would be a pity if the young were to be left with the delusion that brotherly love was an invention of the hippies.

In all our discussions with the young on matters of religious and moral education, we must guard against the kind of seminar which ends up as a sharing of doubts. Although it is only by expressing opinions that the young can formulate their thoughts, there will be some who will only produce destructive opinions and take every opportunity to find fault and to denigrate. While giving due weight to their opinions, we ourselves must never be afraid to state our own faith and the criteria on which we believe moral judgements should be made. Commitment can only be taught by the committed.

What we need in the schools is not less religious instruction or, as I prefer to call it, moral education, but more. Above all, we need the committed teachers who are able to put children in the way of Christ and all He stands for, not only by what they teach but by how they live. Who was it that said, 'What you are speaks so loud that I cannot hear what you say'? Teachers have enormous influence with the young, far more than many of them realize—indeed, it is often frightening to realize how much it is.

I had a letter the other week from a married woman whom I

used to teach in her teens almost twenty years ago. She said to me, 'You must have influenced me far more than I realized at the time because I often find myself quoting you.' I have not the slightest recollection of having said anything at all memorable to her but apparently I did.

I was talking the other day to a headmaster who told me that some little while ago he was puzzled to find a lot of unrest in the senior school and mutterings of pupil-power. As this seemed most unlike the boys concerned, he had a talk with them and was immediately struck by the parrot-fashion in which they repeated what was obviously jargon and not deeply held convictions. Still puzzled, he talked it over with his senior master, quoting some of the stock phrases. These were immediately recognized as the clap-trap talked in the staff-room by a new young master, just down from a university notorious for its student unrest. Fortunately for the school, the man concerned departed quite soon and before any real damage had been done, but one can see from this how impressionable the young can be.

Because of this I believe most profoundly that it is morally wrong for an adult, however sincere and convinced a non-believer he may be, to undermine the religious faith of the young, either by word or by example. I can hear the secularists protesting that this is grossly unjust for it gives an unfair advantage to the supporters of religion. This simply is not true, for in the world today the cards are surely stacked against religion, and those who are trying to bring up children in a religious faith are having to defend every inch of their position against assaults on all sides. The secularists *need* no help—the average child is subjected to a ceaseless bombardment of ideas which say in effect that the worship of mammon is the only worth-while worship. Even if those of us who believe in a Supreme Being (I am not here even talking of the Christian god, for I am well aware that children of a different faith can find in that faith a philosophy which, whether it be simple or profound, will measure up to and satisfy their whole personality and build up a standard of conduct which is ethical in the best sense of the word), even if we *are* merely deluded and the whole thing is just a pack of superstitions, at least we are teaching something *positive*. One of the elderly people who wrote to me said:

> I had a real Christian for my teacher from the first to the sixth
> standard and a home where God was honoured and respected so I
> had two very valuable assets, largely lost today. A boat without a
> rudder drifts aimlessly.

In one school of which I was headmistress, it was the prefects'
privilege to stand behind me on the platform during assembly,
thus facing the school. In the row immediately in front of us
were the eleven-year-olds. I knew that one very strong-minded
young woman in the sixth was an agnostic and, moreover, that
she took no part in the hymns and prayers, for we had discussed
this and I had agreed to it. She came to me one day, considerably shaken. While serving school lunch at the head of a table of
first-formers she had been asked by a small girl, 'Why don't
you say "Our Father" in the mornings? Don't you believe in
Jesus?' It had not occurred to either of us that the little ones
would notice, for most of them stood with their eyes tight shut
during the prayers. This one, obviously, had been peeking! I
asked my young agnostic what she had answered and whether
she had told the truth. Much agitated, she answered, 'Miss
Manners, I *couldn't*! Have you seen their faces when they're
saying their prayers?' I had, of course, and I knew exactly what
she meant.

'Well,' I said, 'what are you going to do about it?'

We talked for some time and the upshot of it was that she
decided that she would have to join in with the rest. She did not
want to give up her place on the platform and slide into the hall
in time for the announcements for she confessed rather guiltily
that she 'got something' from the 'togetherness' of the whole
school and, anyway, the choir was worth hearing, purely from a
musical point of view. I raised an eyebrow and asked if she would
not feel that she was violating her principles, to which she
replied that she did not see that principles were really involved
when you came down to it. It would not do her any harm, she
felt, to repeat meaningless formulae and she quite enjoyed a
good sing anyway. What she was quite clear about was that it

was no part of her duty to herself as an agnostic to injure the faith of a child.

'She'll learn to doubt soon enough,' she went on, 'without me helping on the process.'

That seventeen-year-old showed more genuine concern for children than all the secularists who are bleating about the immorality of exposing the young to religious indoctrination. By all means let us do everything in our power to revitalize the treatment of religion in our schools, but let us not, in the sacred name of freedom, deprive our children of their Christian heritage, and of the support which it can be to them in the difficult task of making value-judgements in this materialistic world.

It is a commonplace to say that religious instruction has for years been the Cinderella subject in our schools. Any member of staff who happened to be free has been dragooned into taking a lesson, regardless of whether he was a committed Christian or not, or even of whether he had any strongly held moral views. Most if not all of these conscripts have objected strongly to the work and their objections have been made manifest in the slipshod lessons which they have given. The fact that, in many schools, R.I. was the first period in the day has been a splendid excuse to spend much of the period on registration, dinner money, milk money and general chat. Nothing could be more obvious to the children than the complete unimportance of the subject.

Even when one reaches the rarefied atmosphere of 'O' levels, it is unusual to find a school which offers Scripture Knowledge as anything more than a soft option to the less able, and I suspect that very few boys' schools offer it at all. To their eternal shame, it is only fairly recently that the universities and professional bodies have accepted an 'O' level pass in this subject as a qualification, and it is still an accepted fact that an 'A' level pass is despised unless the applicant should actually want to read Theology at university.

If there is to be any sort of religious revival in this country—and I do not altogether discount the possibility—then, far from abolishing religious instruction from the schools, we must make every effort to make it a most important part of the curriculum. This is not to say that teachers should take the old authoritarian approach of 'This you must do'; but I believe most profoundly that it should be possible first to teach the simple stories at an early age and then, perhaps from the age of about thirteen onwards, to help children to rethink their earlier impressions in the light of their later knowledge of science and the world around them. They should then be able to think about the great issues confronting mankind, in the light of a background of Scriptural knowledge and of the history of man's groping towards a better understanding of his own nature and his place in the world. It is not beyond the realms of possibility that the Gospels could then be used as a kind of reference-book through which the older pupils might be encouraged to seek the answers to their own personal problems. As Denis Potter's controversial play *Son of Man* showed, even though it was written from the point of view of an agnostic, there is much in the personality of Jesus of Nazareth to appeal to the young today. It is ironic that He should be despised and rejected by the very people who, if one is to believe in their reforming zeal and social conscience, would have been His most ardent followers had they lived two thousand years ago.

Many of those who attack religion in schools do so without ever having been inside a school since their own childhood. I have already admitted that, in many schools, it does more harm than good; and there is no one to blame for this but the teachers and the local authorities who do not insist on adequate provision of specialist teachers in at least as many schools as possible. What an outcry there is because the schools suffer a shortage of mathematics and science specialists! I very much doubt whether anyone even *knows* what sort of provision there is of those properly qualified to undertake the moral education of the young. But very many schools are making a planned and deliberate effort to help young people understand themselves through the study of not only the Christian religion but, at sixth-form level certainly, the other great religions of the world. In an increasingly multiracial school society, the voluntary presence of young people of other obediences during R.I.

periods can be of enormous value. I have always found these children more than willing to join in discussions and to share experiences with the Christians, to the infinite benefit of all.

A recent survey revealed that ninety per cent of parents wanted the continuation of compulsory religious instruction and of the daily assembly in schools. Even if they are to be over-ruled, as seems to happen so often nowadays when our masters know so much better than we do what we want, or rather what is good for us, many schools will, at least for a long time, want to continue along traditional lines. By 'traditional lines', I certainly do not mean what the secularists imagine. It might come as a surprise to them to learn, as they could do quite easily by asking to be present any morning in one of our schools, that for many thousands of children morning assembly is a vital and real experience in their daily lives. Many teachers would be able to give examples of children who, although showing no outward signs of having been in any way affected by a service, will nevertheless at some later date reveal by some chance remark that they have carried away from it an indelible impression of something absolutely relevant to their lives.

I heard a story recently from a colleague which is not without significance. After morning assembly one day, happening to meet a member of her staff, she made some comment about the particular passage which had been read. Miss X looked rather guilty and said, 'As a matter of fact, I don't often listen. I look on assembly as a nice *restful* start to the day.'

I hope that I shall not be looked on as cynical if I say that, for that reason alone, I should be sorry to see it go.

10

Let Them Get On With It!

Are we worrying too much about the young, and was Pamela Fox in the *Daily Mail* right when she took me to task for my 'lofty views'? Her conclusion read:

> Older generations too easily and conveniently forget the more extreme and peculiar tastes of their own youth. If they dropped their morbid fascination with everything the young say and do, and just let them get on with it, the young might not feel so obliged to rebel and shock their so easily shockable elders.

All right, Miss Fox, we 'let them get on with it'. With what? And with what result? Granted that the majority, as I hope we can all still believe, despite all appearances to the contrary, remain decent, normal, steady young people, are we really justified in letting Angela get on with it, whose horrifying photograph must have spoiled the Sunday breakfasts of a good many parents on a fine May morning. Angela is twenty-one and hooked on barbiturates which she injects through her veins. On one of her arms, as the *Sunday Times* photograph showed in hideous close-up, there is a four-inch long gaping wound, the result of a burst abscess caused by filthy needles. The wound had been stitched the previous day, but the stitches were no longer there and Angela could not remember how or when they had been removed. At twenty-one, she has about five years left to live and her death, with fingers and toes already lost through gangrene, is too awful to contemplate.

The doctors at the hospital emphasize that Angela is one of their 'better' cases. At most times of the day two or three addicts can be seen lying unconscious on the floor, and when they regain consciousness their wounds are dressed and they leave. Charing Cross Hospital treats ten to fifteen addicts a day, and the number is increasing. The doctor in charge says, 'There is really no long-term hope for any of them.'

Or do we let the young vandals get on with it? In Manchester there are at least a dozen cases of vandalism in schools each week. Milkbottles are thrown, treacle and flour from the domestic-science room daubed around, windows smashed—'The whole range,' says an official from the education office. The bill for repairs last year was £26,000. And this in a city where the introduction of wholesale comprehensivization in 1967 was supposed to usher in the millennium!

Liverpool's vandalism costs the city £900,000 a year; the G.P.O.'s repair bill rose from £360,000 to £450,000 in one year and the amount of money stolen from kiosks doubled; Camden Borough Council reports: 'The following have been the main targets for vandalism and hooliganism—play centres, public conveniences, street furniture, parking-meters, council estates (lifts, glazing to stairways and landings, light fittings, sheds, trees, shrubs and grassed areas), empty properties awaiting repairs or conversion, building-sites, baths, cemeteries, public halls, library premises and children's homes'; Southend council says that vandalism is getting worse and more vicious. Last year, it is estimated that it cost the country about £3,000,000.

It is not the amount of money which worries me but the state of mind of the young people—and they are mostly young people—whose boredom, vindictiveness, malice, frustration and just plain hatred of society cause them to take revenge in this senseless orgy of destruction. For senseless it is, since many of the things which they destroy have actually been created for their benefit.

Nor is hooliganism confined to what used to be known as 'slum children', for there is plenty of it in the universities. I am not talking of the incidental destruction involved in student protests and sit-ins but sheer, wanton destruction for 'fun'. Akin to this is the flagrant dishonesty in universities nowadays. I was told by a friend in one of the larger redbricks that when students rent a flat they expect to furnish and stock it with goods stolen from halls of residence, refectories and union buildings. Another university has employed library guards for the sole purpose of stopping students from stealing books, a move which has more than paid for the guards' wages in the number of books saved.

Are we to let the young 'get on with it', when the doctors tell us that cases of resistant gonorrhoea are becoming more prevalent and that this disease is the most common in the world after measles? Incidentally, a recent survey of ninety-two women patients revealed that sixty-three would not ever have had extra-marital intercourse had they not been taking the Pill. Do we still want to give birth-control advice in schools and supply the Pill to the unmarried on the National Health?

Are we to let the students 'get on with it' until eventually one of their demos erupts into the sort of bloody violence we saw in Chicago in 1968 and in Kent, Ohio, last year?

I referred in an earlier chapter to the short-story competition run by the *Times Educational Supplement*. I confess to having found the winning entry profoundly disturbing. It is by a fifteen-year-old girl and, as *The Times* rightly says, it is outstanding for sheer economy and power of writing. It is at the same time an entirely revolting story of death, horror and sadism, describing how a class of young children abuse the dead body of their teacher who has collapsed in class, first kicking her until 'the leg was in a mangle of broken skin and dark blood' and, finally, sticking a knife into her glazing eye so that 'a slow trickle of blood curved its way from the corner of her mouth'.

I am not quite sure why *The Times* felt that this deserved first prize—no doubt like those publishers who wish to sell obscene books they justify it by saying that it has literary merit and is 'for the public good'. If this utterly beastly story is the best that school can inspire in the literate young, then something has gone wrong. The young author says that she likes horror stories and horror films (an interesting observation since, at fifteen she is too young to go to X films), and is looking forward to going to London when she leaves school. If she and others like her are simply allowed to 'get on with' their taste for blood and violence, they may find more horror than they have bargained for.

It is precisely because one generation, derided and discouraged by the mass-media, has abdicated responsibility for the next that we are now faced with an attack on society by the young which any sane person must view with alarm. Let us take a look at this rebellion, this war between the generations, and try to come to a few tentative conclusions about it.

In the first place, it is arrant nonsense to pretend that by leaving the young alone we shall deprive them of the urge to rebel. It is precisely because we *have* left them alone, to make their value-judgements as a peer-group, based on the trashy standards of pop culture with its emphasis on instant success without visible effort, that we now find that their idols are delinquent drug-takers who openly boast that the young do as they like. The pathetic thing is that all the time they are 'doing their own thing', in the happy illusion that they are completely free of any kind of adult influence or domination, they are actually being manipulated like a 'puppet on a string' by the adult moguls of the entertainment industry.

The young are not rejecting standards, they need them and are looking for them; but, at the risk of being repetitive, I must emphasize that if *we* do not give them standards, or if they find ours totally unacceptable, then they will find them elsewhere. They cannot find anything of lasting value from their peers, immature, tasteless and half-educated as they are, and all that they are likely to learn from the mass media is that deviant behaviour such as drug-taking, sexual promiscuity and the use of violence as an appropriate means of settling a problem, is the acceptable norm. Yet these restless and rebellious children are growing up all the time and soon they will find that they are not young any more and that the socially hostile attitudes which they have adopted have left them totally unequipped for the adult world. I often wonder what the hippies, whose motto is 'Never trust anyone over thirty', imagine that *they* will be doing when they are that age.

I think we must distinguish between two distinct groups of rebels: first, the intellectually less able whose rebellion, apart from the vandalism of the few, is a fairly passive thing, in that they simply ignore their elders and live in their own world of coffee-bars, discothèques, boutiques, with their pep-pills and reefers, their uniform hair and clothes styles which nevertheless are constantly changing at the dictates of fashion, their hippy vocabulary and their secondhand hippy philosophy of 'happiness' reached through sex, drugs and pop music. They do very little harm except to themselves, but that harm can be fatal, for it would no doubt be in some teenage bar or at some groovy teenage party that Angela first sought excitement or escape in drugs.

Student rebellion, although it obviously has links with the less aggressive teenage culture, is a rather different phenomenon, purely because here we are dealing not with fourteen- or fifteen-year-olds of fairly limited intelligence but with the so-called cream of our educational system, the top five per cent who have had the best that our schools can apparently give them and who, moreover, are young adults even though their behaviour is at times sadly infantile. Basically they are rebelling against the same things as the less articulate, but because their education has at least taught them to read something other than comic books and pop magazines—even though they apparently do so with little discrimination or critical acumen—they have progressed, if that is the word, from the adolescent 'rebel-without-a-cause' stage. They have found a whole series of causes to which they can devote their energies, whether con-structive or—as I am afraid is too often the case, however good their original intentions—destructive. What they do not always realize is that they, just as much as the mindless teenagers, jerking and writhing to the strident beat of *Top of the Pops*, are often being used and manipulated, not this time by commercial string-pullers but by much more sinister agents, the political pressure groups who find student unrest a fertile field in which to sow disorder and anarchy. When the intellectually less able becomes so violent that he has to smash something up, he sets about a football special or a telephone kiosk. These forms of violence would not on the whole be acceptable to the student who does not consider himself delinquent and needs to justify his actions to himself. So he finds his outlet in sit-ins and marches, all with (to him) praiseworthy objects but all equally likely to end in as much mindless violence as the vandalizing of a school or block of council flats.

All these things are inter-related, despite the varying intellec-tual equipment of the different groups—the deliberate alienation from the older generation, a demand for all the privileges hitherto reserved for that generation, money, sex, prestige and ultimately power and the violent means of achieving these ends or of demonstrating dissatisfaction, so it would appear that there is some common cause for their rebellion.

This is much more than a relatively harmless and healthy resentment by the young of the old and a natural feeling that if only the young had their way the world would be transformed into Utopia overnight. I should certainly not want to live in a world where the young were blissfully content, for such a world would be stagnant. Any healthy society can accommodate any amount of dissent, but there is a grave danger in the present situation that the youth culture will totally reject all the values of society, having become altogether too strident, too violent and too dissident. It is not possible to define their rebellion in one sentence, but it might be called a revulsion against the computerization of life.

It is not only the young, and especially the students, who are becoming increasingly frightened of being ground into a system in which they feel themselves to have no say, which they do not understand, but which they are pretty sure they dislike. Over the past decade very many adults have become disillusioned with the processes of democracy and have expressed their dissatisfaction with all the political parties in Mercutio's words: 'A plague o' both your houses!' Is it not significant that South African teams have been visiting this country ever since the war without the violent resentment which the Seventies tours have aroused? It has not taken the public until now to realize that apartheid is an evil thing. It is only the method of protest that has altered. The opposition is being driven out into the streets because they feel that it is useless to protest through the usual democratic and political channels.

I do not believe that the nature of the young is inherently any more noble and full of disinterested humanitarianism than was ours in the Thirties and Forties. Young people are superficially better informed, simply as a result of the mass-media of communications. They know of the existence of what they conceive to be a wrong or an injustice almost as soon as it happens, and with all the impetuosity of youth they want to take immediate action, to rush into battle on a white charger, 'ready to face the danger, ready to right the wrong', even though the danger is no more deadly than a few good-humoured London bobbies, and the only action the totally ineffective one of sitting on a muddy pavement and getting in the way of harmless pedestrians.

If one could wave a magic wand and offer to transport them to the seats of power so that they could implement their solutions to the problems of the atomic threat, Black Power, apartheid, Vietnam, pollution, world hunger and all the other burning questions which arouse in them so much righteous indignation, they would be totally incapable of action, for they *have* no solution—how could they have? The protest is all, and one is forced to the conclusion that all these issues, like the university grievances of political files, iron gates, representation on Senate and so on, are means not ends. The very fact that the 'cause' changes almost overnight would indicate that it is of secondary importance. There is no unification of ends among the rebellious and protesting young but only a unification of means: the march, the sit-in, the demo, disruption and all too often destruction when the delinquent few use legitimate protests as a front for their hooligan activities.

A few weeks ago there appeared in the newspapers the photograph of an anonymous young girl. She could have been one of millions for she looked like all the rest, long hair, thumbs thrust through the belt of her jeans in the true unisex style and a tee-shirt. Across her fashionably flat chest there leapt a black panther and the caption of the photograph was: *Netherlands delegate to European Black Panther Solidarity Committee's conference last weekend in Frankfurt student hostel.* Despite her remarkably anaphrodisiac gear, she was a pretty girl, aged about seventeen, immature, almost innocent. What in the name of God (and I am not blaspheming) does that *child* know of the Black Panthers, of the desperate problems facing America, of the true conditions in South Africa or even the Caribbean? How could she ever begin even dimly to comprehend the agony and the greatness of a woman like Coretta King? Yet there she stands in her silly little-boy uniform, prating about solidarity to an audience of

136

equally ignorant and naïve children, most of whom will hardly ever have spoken to a negro much less seriously discussed with one the grievances and aims of the Black Panthers.

Let us imagine for one moment that there could have been a similar cause in the Thirties. In the first place, no news of it would have been likely to reach the young of many countries or, if it had done, it could not have made the impact that news makes nowadays, with Press and T.V. reporters swooping down like vultures whenever they think there may be violence and especially violence involving the young. Even if a few militant young people had heard about their 'oppressed black brothers', as the Solidarity Committee no doubt calls the Panthers, regardless of slogans like 'Kill Whitey' and 'Burn, baby, burn', they would have had no money with which to go gallivanting all over Europe to conferences and, moreover, would have felt that, even given the money, they could scarcely afford the time, their studies being a pretty full-time job and their meagre grants entirely dependent on their passing their examinations, and on not being sent down, either for poor work or for misbehaviour.

In any case, although the young seem completely unaware of it, we had our cause in the Thirties and it did not vanish overnight because we got bored with it or found a more spectacular one. Like the poor, of which there were some three million in this country alone, our cause was always with us and it frightened the living daylights out of us. We *knew* who our enemies were: they had names and faces and we could see them on the newsreels and listen to their terrifying ranting on the radio. We did not indulge in childish petulance and refuse to play games with the Nazis. We sent our teams to the Olympic Games and listened to the frightening rhythmic chant of '*Deutschland! Deutschland!*' Not only did we know who our enemies were, we knew that one day soon we should have to stand up and face them, frightened and ill-armed though we were. The young talk as though 'living under the shadow of the Bomb' were an excuse for every kind of idiocy. It never occurs to them that *we* were just as frightened. When war was declared in 1939, I am sure that I was not alone in expecting the country to be wiped off the map of Europe with bombs and poison gas.

137

•

Of course, it did not happen but that is beside the point. *We thought it would and lived all through our teens with that thought uppermost in our minds.* We had our Vietnam, but it was called Spain and many of our friends died there. Guernica was our Sharpeville, only it was for real, not a fancy dress masquerade in Trafalgar Square ten years after the event.

Then, with the coming of war, the cause and the enemy were even more clearly defined, even though some of our comrades took rather a long time making up their minds which side they were on, since Russia had signed a non-aggression pact with the Nazis. For most of us, however, there was no such dubiety. With absolutely no illusions about its being sweet to die for one's country and a pretty strong suspicion that that was exactly what we were going to do before very long, we stood up and fought. Apparently so that the present generation could have freedom to sit down and protest!

Unfair to the young? Well, maybe—but it is high time that someone told them that their generation has no monopoly of courage, compassion, commitment. We did not spend our youth fighting imaginary ideological battles on the plains of Grosvenor Square. Imperfect though the world certainly is, we did the best we could when we sweated and worked to build it, and if we had been as craven and uncaring as the young seem to want to believe, it would have been a sorry world indeed.

The fact that more young people appear to be concerned with humanitarian movements proves nothing, therefore, about their alleged superiority to the young of the first half of this century. All it illustrates is what we already know, namely, that for purely technical reasons they are better informed, and that they are geographically more mobile and financially more powerful. Their bogey-men have not the reality of ours and neither has the action they take against them.

If a generation which faced a real threat, not in far-off countries or imaginary futures but in their own cities and homes, finds it difficult to sympathize with the young and their hastily invented and as hastily discarded excuses for discontent, we must not, however, dismiss this discontent as totally groundless and unjustified. There are deep underlying causes, probably hardly comprehended or even acknowledged by the young themselves, and if we are to go any distance at all towards solving the problems, we must try to unearth these buried fears and understand them, for, as I have said, they are partly our fears too.

Life—simply being alive—has somehow become a less than satisfactory state of affairs for millions of people in this and, no doubt, in many other countries. A few people are the lucky ones, not because they have a lot of money, for very often they are poorly paid, relatively speaking, but because the activity which occupies the major part of their lives—their work—is intensely satisfying to them and they enjoy doing it. There must have been a time when a large proportion of the working population got considerable joy from their work, even though much of it was hard and not very well rewarded materially. But the skilled men, the craftsmen who could see a job well done and some-thing of beauty and worth created by their hands, must surely have got much more than a mere living in terms of money from their work. They were living *in* their work and were able to have pride in it and hand down their skills to their sons.

Even the many who did humbler work did it in small groups and enjoyed some sort of relationship with their employers which, patronizing though it probably was on the one side and servile on the other, nevertheless was a *human* relationship between real people. If you resented the master in the big house, at least you knew who it was you resented, you could put a name and a face to the object of your resentment, you could even spit surreptitiously in the dust as he walked past in mill or factory or farm! Most people did not have a lot of money but neither did they need a lot of money. They were too occupied in getting the necessities of life to envy those who had the luxuries. Luxuries were for leisure and working people had precious little of that.

This situation has been changing for a very long time but never faster than in the last thirty years. We now have a working population (and of that population the young are the most affluent for they have most of their money to spend on themselves), in which most people are bored to distraction with their work. What is the aim of large numbers of craftsmen nowadays? To win the pools and never work again. Able-bodied men live on National Assistance because they cannot earn very much more in a job, and see no point in working if they can get a living—the sole object of working—without. In the Thirties, when men were on the dole, it was the idleness more than the poverty which was the soul-destroying thing. Only forty years ago, working men *wanted* to work, not only because they needed the money but because work fulfilled some basic need. This is far from being the case today, for men have become machine-minders and they feel themselves to be of less value in real terms than the machines they mind, for men are more easily replaced. Work has got nothing to do with real life which only begins when the factory hooter goes—life is lived on 'Saturday night and Sunday morning', in the pub and club, at the dogs, football and bingo, or if you are young at the coffee-bar and discothèque. Life is leisure and having fun and the only reason for working is to get more money to spend on more fun. Until the fun becomes as boring as the work and you look for your kicks elsewhere, in vandalism, football hooliganism, sex and drugs.

If you dislike your job, then you are going to dislike the 'Boss'—but who is the boss in these gigantic, international concerns where so many millions spend their forty-hour week, fifty weeks a year? Whom do you hate in Imperial Chemical Industries or General Motors? The answer is the System, especially if you have picked up a few Marxist catch-phrases from one of the comrades, and from that it is only a step to a general alienation from society and certainly from political parties who all strike you as being as bad as each other, only concerned with taking from you in taxes the money which you ought to be able to spend on having fun.

Another cause of unease in British society today is un-doubtedly our decline as a world power. However much the young may say that they abhor the old imperial ideas, there is a deep sense of deprivation hidden somewhere inside them because we cut so little ice in the world. They sneer at the old-fashioned heroic virtues yet desperately need heroes, as witness the ardour with which they fall for any personality-cult which the manipulators dangle before them—Che Guevara, Ho Chi Minh, the Black Panthers, and, of course, the Jaggers and Lennons of their tawdry pop world. Ever since the first tribe painted its young with woad and sallied forth to knock the stuffing out of the tribe in the next valley, as the young have come of age, they have put on their uniforms and marched to war, to 'where the action is', the 'scene', the 'happening'. There has never been any need for the young, bursting with health, vigour, exuberance and animal spirits, to invent happenings; life (and death) was happening all around them all the time. Until now. So they make their own wars and the excitement that goes with war, in aggro and demos, frenzied dancing, sex and L.S.D.

Everyone, young as well as old, has an increasing feeling of powerlessness. It is probably true to say that the mass of the people always have been powerless, but here again it is a matter of knowing or not knowing in whose power you are. If you were a serf under some Norman baron, or a downtrodden peasant in pre-revolutionary France, you knew who had the power all right. Also, nobody pretended to you that you were anything *but* powerless, you had not the inestimable privilege of putting a cross on a paper every five years in order to decide which of two tyrants should lay the lash about your long-suffering shoulders.

We live in a democracy and in a world where we have largely democratic allies. In theory, we are the captains of our souls, the masters of our fate. And that is the biggest laugh of the century, only it is not really very funny. The young do not find it so, anyway. All around us, in our own cities, our own country and all around the world, things are happening which we mortally detest but we are absolutely powerless to do anything to stop them. The political scene is infinitely depressing. When we look at the two major parties, we seem to find a common core of similar policies which nobody in the country supports but which are being inflicted upon us for our own good by our masters; and then on either side of this common ground, as it were, are policies so opposite that whichever party wins, half the country is bound to be reduced to impotent rage by the bland assumption of the winners that they have a mandate to impose these policies on the whole country. And unless our M.P.

dies or resigns, we shall have no hope of doing even the smallest thing to alter that state of affairs for the next five years. This system is called democracy, and I cannot think of a better one offhand, but the way it is operating at present makes one wonder why so many millions have thought it worth dying for. Is it any wonder that so many disillusioned young people have decided that it is better to be red than dead?

Nor is the situation improved in Britain by the economic straits in which we as a nation obstinately remain. Whatever we are told, we do not understand the nature of the crisis, we are simply left with the conviction that we are at the mercy, not even of men and governments, but of blind, economic forces which *no one* can understand or control, a conviction which intensifies our feelings of helplessness, of frustration and resentment. If the adults feel like this—and I am afraid that very large numbers of us do—how much more violently will the young react, for they at least have a ready-made scapegoat— our generation. We can only blame the anonymous gnomes of Zürich without having the least idea who they are or if they even exist at all. The young can—and do—blame us, as witness my violent young attacker: 'It's your generation that polluted the Earth, it's your generation that's responsible for all the strife in the world today.'

The world we live in and in which the young are forming their values has become too big and frightening, too machine-dominated and impersonal, for any one individual to feel that he can make a significant contribution to it. He feels instinctively that he is being exploited and manipulated even though he cannot quite see how or by whom, and he vents his sullen resentment of *Them* in wild-cat strikes, petty dishonesty and law-breaking, income-tax fiddling and the rest. In 1968 the amount stolen in this country was £51,000,000 and only £9,000,000 was recovered. In the same year British Rail discovered 20,000 ticket frauds—how many went undiscovered? One in fourteen television holders did not buy a licence. And so the dreary catalogue of resentful behaviour continues.

The young, having more energy, react more violently but the underlying discontents are similar.

Professor Max Beloff writing in *The Times* spoke of his fears of a new 'Dark Age' in the universities, when 'we shall have to look to some new version of the monastery to keep alive the torch of learning until the next Renaissance'. Although I hesitate to disagree with someone who is clearly much more in touch with the universities than I am, I nevertheless feel that he is perhaps painting too gloomy a picture. We obviously cannot pretend that all is well on the university campus, any more than we can close our eyes to the greasers and skinheads in the slum streets, but it would be a great pity if the general public became actively hostile to the whole idea of a university because of the behaviour of a very small minority.

For, let there be no mistake about it, the disaffected among the university population are very few indeed and they are almost without exception active members of some far-to-the-left political association: international Marxists, international socialists, communists, downright anarchists. These are the people who have no interest whatsoever in reforming either the university society or society in general, who want nothing less than destruction and the chance to build their own left-wing utopia in the ruins. That none of them is competent to build a henhouse is a matter of small importance to them. They make their impudent demands in the name of all the students although not even the most blatant rigging of ballots and suppressing of opposition in Union meetings can disguise the fact that the only people whom they represent are themselves. It is not even likely that anyone in Moscow or Peking would want to admit to followers such as the two hundred from the London School of Economics who shuffled around London for two hours on May Day, trying in vain to get someone—*anyone*—to join in their 'protest against victimization and repression'. The utter unreality of their aspirations was clearly demonstrated in their approach to some building workers with cries of 'Brothers, come and join us'. The replies of the workers are unquotable, I am afraid! Their parrot-cries of 'Smash the bourgeoisie!' and 'Down with capitalism!' caused hoots of derision wherever their mournful cortège wended its way. One of them claimed that they were representing the oppressed of the world. If the oppressed have no better hope than these young idiots, then their plight is sore indeed.

These are the professional trouble-makers who spend their time and their Government grants running around the country from one university to another, stirring up unrest of the most violent kind. They are quite unscrupulous and will resort to any lie or illegal act to further their own ends. They make demands but do not really want them to be acceded to, for only with a continuing sense of grievance will they be able to foment the revolution which is their aim. If truthful answers are given to their trumped-up questions, such as that there are no political files in a particular university, their reply is that the authorities are lying. If the Vice-Chancellor makes the mistake of acceding to their impudent demands, he does not find that he has bought peace or even a truce, for the next demand will be even more outrageous. Much of their behaviour, if indulged in outside the confines of the university, would undoubtedly lead to criminal charges, as some of them found to their cost when they attacked a Cambridge hotel and others tried to blow up a bank. They are quite blatantly using the freedom and protection afforded to them by the university to destroy the very institution which protects them.

Not content with trying to destroy academic values, free speech and free inquiry in the universities, this activist minority wants to get its grubby hands on schoolchildren. It is difficult to imagine anything more irresponsible than the action of the Oxford undergraduates who paraded about outside city secondary schools, handing out birth-control literature to the children as they came out. I do not know what sort of reception they got from the children, but the Essex students who called upon girls from my school to demand pupil-power and throw off the tyranny of their teachers got a very cold shoulder. The girls told me later that they had found the arguments of the students incoherent and their pamphlets illiterate, and that anyway, all of the freedoms which they were being urged to fight for had for long enough been commonplace in our school.

This was much the reaction of some sixth form girls from a Norwich school when they went to report on a student demo for their school magazine. They seriously wanted to know what the students were protesting about and asked them serious questions, only to be answered with shouted slogans and the same old Marxist parrot-cries which were old-fashioned in the Twenties. The girls gave up in disgust, saying that it was impossible to get any sense out of them.

Undoubtedly, one of the non-events of the whole student protest scene was the famous occasion when the B.B.C. got together, at some considerable expense, all the so-called 'leaders' from all over Europe, including the egregious Danny the Red. At the time, I was inclined to condemn the B.B.C. for so encouraging these loud-mouthed militants by giving them publicity. On watching the pitiful performance which they put up, I began to credit the B.B.C. with positively Machiavellian subtlety, for nothing was more calculated to discredit these sawdust conspirators than the simple act of asking them, in front of millions of viewers, to say in simple language just what they wanted and what, given the power they were seeking, they would do with it. The result, as all those who watched will remember, was pathetic. I found myself feeling sorry for the poor children . . . almost.

Apart from the purely political demands of the real activists who want to tear down, blow up, destroy the whole university as a symbol of the hated capitalist system which is providing their grants, what are the other causes of concern on campus, leaving aside the international issues such as Vietnam, and now Cambodia? Incidentally, it is difficult to see what British students expect their universities to be able to *do* about these issues, but they are ingenious, to say the least, in the way they manage to prove the guilt of their teachers for what is going on thousands of miles away. Lord Salisbury and Dr Adams have been found unacceptable by some students because of their alleged sympathy for Rhodesia; now Oxford students have ransacked the estates office of the University Chest and claim that Oxford is battening on their black brothers in South Africa by holding shares in De Beers. It is to be hoped that it never becomes the student 'in' thing to protest *against* Welsh and Scottish nationalism rather than for it, otherwise we shall obviously see Vice-Chancellors attacked for owning corgis or Skye terriers!

It seems pretty clear that Cambodia, or whatever the current cause may be, is the focal point for unrest which goes much deeper. One desperately deplores the shooting by the National Guard in Kent, Ohio, of four young people and the wounding of many others, but the bitter fact has to be swallowed that when dissent turns to destruction and violence, then disaster will surely follow. One reads of petrol bombs being found near the six-million-pound computer operated by New York University after occupying students had vacated the building. Is this—this planned destruction of a *computer*—a possible clue to the malaise of the intelligent young? I believe that in the first place the students, like the rest of us, are frustrated and frightened by the power and the impersonality of the system for which and by which they feel they are being processed like so many battery chickens.

In different parts of the world there are different specific fears. In France, the students feel that their work is pointless because there are obviously not going to be enough jobs for them all when they graduate, and although de Gaulle is no longer the hated dictator-figure of 1968, nevertheless the Gaullist régime is little changed. Neither has the extremely unsatisfactory examination system.

In America, hatred of the war in Vietnam springs from a very real fear of being drafted into the army to fight there. Whether their confidence was justified or not, the young saw in the Kennedy brothers a hope for a better America and a better world. That hope seems to them to have died with Robert Kennedy, and they feel driven to desperation by what is now done in their name. Their problem is the reverse of ours. We suffer because our nation is no longer able to be a force for good in the world; the Americans are ashamed and deeply disturbed at their nation's failure to use its power as liberal-minded people feel that it should be used. The My Lai massacre, the political assassinations, the bloody battles of the ghettoes, the Chicago riots—all these things have shaken the people of 'God's own country' to the core, and the young, always most easily roused,

146

feel that there is something very wrong with a system which permits such happenings in the richest and most powerful country in the world.

In Britain, the students only experience these feelings at second hand, which is perhaps why some of us find it difficult to take them as seriously as they would like. It really is completely pointless for British students to protest against the war in Vietnam since there is absolutely nothing that the British Government and people can do about it. Perhaps if there were, the young would feel less bitter. One is forced to the conclusion that, of all the students in the world, the British have less to protest about than any. The Czech and Hungarian students threw their petrol bombs at Russian tanks, not at computers or banks which could not fire back. The enemy selected by students in our country would seem to be the universities themselves, and in most cases, betrayed by fifth columnists in their own ranks and beset with the prevailing adult uncertainty about motives, these have proved a pretty feeble foe.

There are probably some sound reasons for the students' dissatisfaction with the universities but—and here I know that I am asking to be sniped at by those who never fail to leap to the defence of all of the young, even of those who celebrated the twenty-fifth anniversary of the liberation of Holland from the Germans by conducting an orgy of senseless destruction in Amsterdam on 5 May 1970—I am quite unrepentant in my opinion that those who find that they do not like what the university has to offer should get out.

From the very outset, the attitude of many of the university authorities has been craven to the point of idiocy. When the first demand for student power was made in 1967, following student riots in Germany, Japan, America and France, the answer to the militants should have been: No one asked you to come here, you are here on money which you have not earned, there are thousands of young people who would give anything to be where you are now, so if you do not like what we have to offer and are not prepared to take it on our terms, get out. At that time I believe that the majority of students wanted no part in the antics of a few and, if it had been made clear there and then that the authorities would not tolerate politically activated violence by members of the Radical Student Alliance and Revolutionary Students' Federation, the vandalism and general thuggery which have disgraced so many of our universities since then might never have happened. Where the liberal-minded authorities made the mistake was in supposing that the protesters wanted to reform the universities, whereas their real aim was and still is to destroy them and put in their place some utopian fantasy called a 'comprehensive polyversity', with no entrance requirements and no examinations, where one sits around for three years at the public expense discussing plans for the Third World, whatever that may turn out to be.

Like the rest of the adult population, the Vice-Chancellors have allowed themselves to be brainwashed into the belief that the young are much more mature and responsible than they were when young, and so, even beginning to doubt the validity of the academic values which they have always thought it their duty to uphold, they concede that there might be some justice in the claims for participation and so the pass has been sold.

Why, if the original trouble-makers were so few and so obviously concerned with political rather than academic aims, have they not been disowned by the moderate majority? Indeed, why have we seen so many of the moderates actually joining forces with those whom they would have condemned a few years ago? In the first place, it is because they do not really want to get involved but simply want to be left alone to work for their degrees and enjoy as much peace and quiet as the rioters will allow them to have. When they come out in sympathy it is because they feel that they have reasons to be dissatisfied with life at the university, even though their reasons may not be those of the militants.

The valid reasons for student disillusionment and discontent have been explored much more fully than is possible for me, by those more closely in touch with the universities, notably Dr Bryan Wilson in his recent book *The Youth Culture and the Universities*. It is therefore difficult to find anything original to say on the subject. Looking at the problem from the side of the schools, however, one gets the feeling that many young people go up to the universities, primed by their teachers who are still living in memories of the dreaming spires of their youth, expecting a wonderful world of learning and culture where they will walk the groves of Academe arm in arm with Socrates. What do they find? A swarming colony of ants housed largely in glass and concrete towers, where they queue for indifferent food in refectories which are third-rate cafeterias, live in shabby digs miles from the university and attend lectures in anonymous droves—or do not attend them and find that nobody cares. Instead of Socrates, they find a Professor whom they only recognize on the rare occasions when they meet him because they have seen his face on television. Many of the younger lecturers are hardly older than the students and seem much more concerned with complaining about their salaries and how iniquitous it is that their elderly 'Prof' hangs on to his chair instead of making way for younger men.

Perhaps the students may have a tutor, and if they come from a properly organized school they will associate this name with the sixth-form master who, for their last two or three years at school, saw them every day, directed their studies, gave them advice on everything from the filling in of U.C.C.A. forms to how to make up a quarrel with the girl-friend and took a genuine and affectionate personal interest in them. Too often, in these enormous factories which are the result of increasing the student population without proper thought as to the needs of the increased numbers, the undergraduate finds that his tutor is a shadowy personage who asks him to an annual Sherry party where the bonhomie is as false as the labels on the wine-bottles.

If he comes from a home and a school that have taught him to value civilized standards of living and behaviour, he will be bewildered and repelled by much that he sees. I remember being shown into a lift by a tutor in a large tower block in the Manchester students' village. All the paper on the walls beside the lift was hanging off in long strips, having been deliberately and neatly cut with a razor or penknife and peeled down. My companion apologized for the graffiti inscribed indelibly with felt pens and lipsticks inside the lift, and I think that we both felt some embarrassment in standing in such close proximity to scribbled obscenities for five floors. The point that struck me about this was that nobody seemed to care—at any rate, nothing apparently was done either to remove the evidence of vandalism or to prevent its recurrence.

I do not think that I am being smug or self-righteous in claiming that the schools from which students come do not suffer from this kind of behaviour, or if they do they tackle the problem pretty smartly. What then happens between school and university?

One can hardly blame students who find themselves insignificant and anonymous names on a vast nominal roll kept by a computer in the administration buildings if they conclude that university, of which they had hoped such great things, has let them down. I am not maintaining that it is the fault of the universities: far from it. Like everyone else engaged in education nowadays, they are trying to make bricks without straw. Expansion has been forced upon them just as secondary re-organization has been forced on the schools, by a Government that either cannot or will not provide the money without which all these grandiose plans will only end in chaos. Just as comprehensive schools are being created with sixth forms for which there are no graduate teachers, so the universities are seeking desperately for qualified lecturers—at the expense of the schools, of course. Men are being employed as lecturers who would hardly have got a post in a grammar school in the Thirties. They have little appreciation of scholarship and, in some cases, openly despise those who have. They work a nine-to-five day for the money and that is that. It is largely from the ranks of these young men, living in picturesque squalor with a trendy wife and a couple of progressively brought-up (i.e., completely undisciplined) children, that the students find their champions in their revolt. If the senior members of the university are so bogged down with the gigantic task of administrating the enormous business concerns which universities have unfortunately become and therefore have no time to get to know the students, the latter are left to the tender mercies of these younger men who, being totally unsuited for the positions they hold, are equally discontented and ready to make common cause with the dissidents.

From all this spring the utterly unrealistic and extravagant demands for participation which, if acceded to, would assuredly usher in the Dark Ages which Professor Beloff fears. Another academic, Professor James of Leeds, has pointed out in a witty letter to *The Times* that in the second century Aulus Gellius castigated students thus: 'Nowadays these fellows who turn to philosophy on a sudden, not content with being wholly without purpose, without learning and without scientific training, even lay down the law as to how they are to be taught.' As Professor James goes on to say, we face nothing new; but after Gellius, the Dark Ages *did* ensue.

I am absolutely in sympathy with the students when they ask (though they have no God-given right to *demand*, much less to demand with menaces as they are doing) that they should be allowed involvement in decisions concerning their own environment. Wherever the students' direct experience is relevant— i.e., in matters of welfare, accommodation, medical services, facilities both for work and recreation and, to a large extent, discipline—there should be the closest collaboration between senior and junior members of the university. The authorities should be prepared to listen to the students and discuss with them the diversifying of courses because, although their juniors are painfully young and immature, what they have to say may be worth hearing.

But that is where the capitulation will have to stop if the universities are to survive as transmitters of knowledge. It is arrant nonsense to claim, as the activists do, that students have the right to sit on Senate and Council and to determine academic policy, appoint staff, plan for the future, even years ahead, and dispose literally of millions of pounds. A university has been defined as a place for the meeting of minds and the training of intellects. In it the undergraduate, even the newly qualified graduate, must realize that he is only a beginner and, of course, a transient. If the new B.A. or B.Sc. has learned anything in his three years at university, it should be that he has only just mastered the basic concepts of his discipline whose frontiers are infinity. Students in their first year, even sixth-formers before they go up to university, are now making the nonsensical demand that they should decide on the syllabus which they are to study. It would be interesting to select from the militants one undergraduate from each faculty, or even to be fair a small committee of them, and let them get on with the practical task of drawing up a degree syllabus for each of their disciplines. They would hardly know where to begin.

I remember talking not so long ago to the Vice-Chancellor of a university, a distinguished scientist but one who has spent many years in administrative work, away from his subject. He told me ruefully that he had been looking at the Final Honours papers in his subject at his old university. Not only, he said, could he not have done them today but he could *never* have done them, because much of the knowledge being examined had not been discovered when he was an undergraduate. If the frontiers of knowledge are widening at such a rate, how can any young-ster only just out of school possibly hope to know sufficient to be able to determine curricula?

Neither can the student possibly have the experience of the world and of human nature, much less the business acumen, to serve effectively on policy-making bodies. Senate and Council consist of men with long experience of the matters with which they are dealing. Student members would probably not be appointed until their Finals year, which would give them a term of office of one year. The mind boggles at the fantastic amount of time that would be wasted, explaining to the 'new boy' what everybody was talking about and what were the principles involved in the business under discussion. Besides which, would any serious student want to spend hours on committee work in the year when he should be giving all his attention to his Finals? Yet he could not possibly have the feel of the place and enough knowledge of anything at all to be the slightest use on a committee of major importance before his third year.

There is the further point that no student could possibly represent anything but a small minority, almost certainly those holding relatively extreme views. One of the reasons why the activists seem to have had it all their own way on the campus is because the moderates—by far the majority—do not attend the union meetings where these ridiculous motions are carried; they are too absorbed in their studies and cannot be bothered to get involved in student politics. If students were given representation on committees which had to discuss the really serious business of university government and policy, we should see the absurd situation of some glib Trotskyite or Maoist 'elected' by a couple of hundred others like him at a meeting which no one except the revolutionary few attended. He would then bore the senior members of the committee to death and waste an incredible amount of time, lecturing them with platitudes about the bourgeoisie and the workers and all the claptrap which they grew out of before he was born. In any case, the left-wing student movement has so many splinter groups and spends so much time quarrelling among its members over abstruse points of dogma that it is difficult to believe that it would muster sufficient unanimity to elect a representative.

I am not therefore particularly inclined to take student rebellion seriously in Britain. As the *Times Educational Supplement* says in its leader of 8 May 1970: 'Where American students take up real causes and defend them against tear-gas and clubbing, British students grope for a plausible excuse for a demo—iron gates, political files, university governors with South African connections—and end by singing "Auld Lang Syne" with the police. . . . On the big questions, student protest here has been a shadow-play of the American drama.'

It is encouraging to see that the moderates are at last standing up to be counted and seemingly realizing that if they hold aloof any longer, thus allowing the wreckers to have it all their own way, the whole student body may be the sufferer in the law-and-order backlash. I was at a northern university in the spring of last year and was told of how an earnest young woman student came back to the campus in tears from a door-to-door mission collecting for some very worthy student charity. She had collected precisely nothing except a very great deal of verbal abuse from the townsfolk, who were sick and tired of reading in their newspaper or watching on the 'telly' the clownish antics at one university after another. The British may not be over-fond of their politicians—even though they do not, as the French do, use the word as a term of abuse—but they have a strong instinct for fair play and free speech and draw the line at hearing of their Foreign Secretary howled down, with shouts of 'Resign, you bum!' and 'Hang the murderer!', by Oxford undergraduates. If at any time within the last two or three years a political party had appealed to the nation with the platform of 'Stop the students' grants', they would have romped home. And this is a pity.

So it is with relief that one reads at last of the Students' Union at Sussex revoking the illiberal policy steamrollered through by the radicals which effectually prevented free speech on the campus. When some militants were suspected of arson at Keele University, there was mass support for the authorities and a student spokesman went on record as saying that there was no serious unrest there. After the despicable events at the Oxford Union, the President, to his eternal credit, expressed himself as 'bitterly ashamed'.

Everyone feels shock and sadness at the death of four students in Kent, Ohio, but perhaps the silly boys and girls in this country and, for that matter, in America too, who have been mouthing their idiotic platitudes about revolutionary confrontations and so on, will now realize that there is no such thing as a bloodless revolution. Sooner or later, if the confronters throw enough stones and petrol bombs at armed police or National Guardsmen, somebody is killed. These pathetically deluded young people seem to imagine that if they shout their slogans long enough and loudly enough, the capitalist system will topple like the walls of Jericho at the sound of Joshua's trumpets of rams' horns. At the cost of four young lives, they have learned that this is not so. Let us hope that there is an end to this madness without British students having to die to stop it.

Nevertheless, even though one discounts the senseless agitation of the radicals, one is left with the uneasy feeling that the moderates would have made their presence felt before now, if everything in the university garden had been lovely. A generation of students has arrived in the universities from homes with no experience of academic life. They have expected everything and, in too many cases, have been given very little. This is the problem which the universities must face, not the trumped-up issues which are the apparent causes of unrest. I do not for one moment advocate compromise with the destroyers nor even an outright acceptance that the students are right to demand participation, but something must be done if the new universities and the expanded older ones are not to break down under intolerable internal stresses which will create conditions in which it will simply be impossible to work.

What none of us can do, whether we concern ourselves with the young in our universities and schools or with those whose lives are divided between their boring work and their equally boring leisure, is follow the *Mail* columnist's advice and simply let them get on with it. The girl Alison, clutching her stray kitten, lying dead on the campus of Kent State University, deserved better than **that.**

11

Bridging the Gap

This then is the problem; and once again let us beware lest we get it out of proportion. There is very little wrong with the vast majority of the younger generation. In some ways they *are* better than we were, but not because of any inherent nobility of character, and there is not the slightest reason why we should praise them for advantages which we have given them.

It is nothing to *their* credit that they have incomparably better educational opportunities than we had, that they are relatively affluent whereas we grew up in the grip of economic stringency, that they have increased mobility and ease of communication in a world made small by jet engines, television and earth satellite. All of these advantages from which spring their heightened awareness of the needs of the world and their response to those needs were the result of the discoveries, the hard work, the inventive genius of our generation, not of theirs. Without us, they would have nothing and be nothing.

Let us never forget this and, just once in a while, let us tell the young so. Let us stop being afraid of them and ashamed of ourselves. Whatever problem there is, it is of our making and it is we and not the young who must solve it. I am convinced that if we take the initiative and make a positive stand for what we believe in, we shall find that we have some unexpected allies: the majority of the young themselves. I realize that the 600-plus letters which I received do not constitute a Gallup poll and that it may be dangerous to draw too firm conclusions from them, but the fact remains that they revealed an enormous hidden reserve of sound, moderate opinion among young people in their teens and twenties, all of them, moreover, welcoming a lead from a determined adult with a sense of values.

There remains the minority, and it is a very dangerous minority indeed. Many are only a danger to themselves and to others of their generation—I am thinking here of the drug-addicts who will certainly be dead before they are thirty but not before they may have infected many others with their own death-wish. The skinheads, though a highly unpleasant phenomenon, nevertheless form a tiny percentage of the population and, on the whole, the authorities will always be able to cope. Vandalism is another matter, and something has got to be done to channel the destructive urges of bored children into other outlets.

The greatest danger to this country, as to America and elsewhere, lies in the threat to freedom and democracy inherent in much of student protest. The tide of protest, confrontation, demonstration which is sweeping the cities of the world may, if it continues to gather momentum, sweep away not the embattled citadels of oppression and privilege which are its targets but the liberties which it has taken the Western world hundreds of years to win. Governments cannot tolerate *ad nauseam* the sort of dissent which more and more frequently explodes into destructive violence. Nor will the general public allow them to. There are signs everywhere of a hardening of attitudes towards student demonstrators. The Benjamin Spocks and Vanessa Redgraves of this world may make their speeches applauding the demos and lay their wreaths in Grosvenor Square, but the ordinary man in the street is sick to death of the sight, sound and thought of demonstrations.

Already there are straws in the wind: even in 1968, the French student revolutionaries got a very dusty answer from the workers whom they tried to recruit and, recently, students had to be rescued by the hated 'pigs' from the wrath of New York building workers. It is a mercy that the teams which South Africa wanted to send here play the relatively 'upper-class' games of rugby and cricket. If they had sent a soccer team I am very much afraid that this country would have seen violence on an unprecedented scale because the average man would have risen in wrath against any attempt to interfere with his divine right to watch football matches. It would have been the demonstrators and not the Springboks who would have needed police protection. It is a shocking yet perfectly comprehensible fact that large numbers of people both here and in the United

States have greeted the tragic death of the Kent students with the observation: 'They had it coming to them', and many reporters, including that most humane of men Alistair Cooke, have commented sympathetically on the plight of the young National Guardsmen, standing for hours facing a horde of jeering, spitting, rock-throwing, obscenity-screaming students, until, finally and understandably, their nerve broke.

We are told that the disgusting scenes at the Oxford Union were the first shot in an organized campaign by revolutionaries led by Robin Blackburn, the lecturer who all but ruined L.S.E. with his pernicious propaganda, to prevent any member of the late Government from speaking in public. This he had publicly stated on B.B.C. radio to be the aim of his movement. One does not know why the Conservatives have been spared his ministrations, but no doubt they will get their turn now. The Member of Parliament who debated with Blackburn in the broadcast dropped a very strong hint that this sort of interference with the democratic system in this country could not be tolerated much longer, and there must be millions who will agree with him. A Socialist Government was clearly afraid to take the repressive measures which will be needed if this sort of anarchy continues. A Conservative government will probably be strong enough though just as reluctant; but, sooner or later, unless the activists see the writing on the wall and switch their tactics in self-preservation, the Government of the day will be forced by public opinion to take action. Wolf Rilla's television play *The Greater Good* had a horribly prophetic persuasiveness. I cannot imagine Britain declining into a police state quite so rapidly as he forecast, but I do believe it to be well within the bounds of possibility that there should, in the not too distant future, be such a law-and-order backlash that we shall wake up one day to find that we no longer have the right of peaceful demonstration and dissent. From this it is only a small step to imprisoning the dissenters and known trouble-makers.

If the older generation really rise in wrath against the young, then pity help the latter, because their elders have all the big guns—literally. Of course, one cannot even visualize a situation where the rebellious young would be actually shot down—at least, one could not have done so before Kent, Ohio. But there are so many ways in which the poor, silly children could be victimized and rendered totally impotent. The futility of many of their actions is amply illustrated in their calls for strikes in the universities. Who are they supposed to be striking against, since no one employs them and their work is of no value to anyone but themselves?

I know that many of them loftily declare that they are making a valuable contribution to society by studying at university, but this is just so much eyewash. They will make a contribution, more or less valuable according to their individual worth, when they enter a profession, but until that time their contribution is nil. Many if not all of their lecturers would not be at all disturbed if the students did not turn up to lectures for a few days. They would merely devote more time to their research, which will be of equal, if not greater, value to the community than the lectures they give. Any rebellious student could be finished with the stroke of a pen if the Local Education Authority (it does not even depend on the Government) stopped paying his grant. If, under such circumstances, his parents turned him out and the Ministry of Social Security refused him National Assistance, he might be in a sorry plight, for what employer, already up to the neck in labour troubles, would give a job to a known troublemaker, fit for nothing, in any case, but unskilled labour?

Now I am not for one moment advocating such draconian methods, but am merely pointing out that such powers are already in the hands of the authorities without any emergency legislation. The power-drunk fanatics who trade on the tolerance of the ordinary man and shelter under the democratic protection of Western countries might do well to remember that even the most long-suffering worm may turn and things in Britain have just about reached the turning-point. In America, one prays that they are not already beyond it, and that the country has not become ungovernable by democratic methods.

This then is why I say that it is time to call a halt, not only to our tolerance of the dangerous lunatics who would destroy democracy but also to our lack of responsibility, as parents and teachers and as a nation, to so many of our young people. I have tried to show in the foregoing chapters the evils which surround the young and the terrible consequences for many of them if they are not given the arms with which to withstand all the wiles of the Devil. If the young people of this country are not to become the victims of unscrupulous agitators and go the way of the American young with their terrible delinquency and drug problems, it is up to us to see that their tremendous social conscience be encouraged and put to good use rather than frustrated and denied. Before the generation gap becomes unbridgeable and the world is faced with a confrontation between two hardened sections of opinion—a confrontation in which, as I have already shown, the young are bound to be the losers—men and women of tolerance and common sense must express the truth with courage and power: that there has probably never been a time in the history of the world when the young needed more firm and loving guidance than they do today, nor a time when it was more necessary for those of us who care to stand up in audible opposition to those influences—and those individuals—who would corrupt not only our children but the nation and the civilized world.

Everyone seems concerned that something should be done, but far too many of us have lost confidence in our ability to do something or even in our right to do it. All of us who deal with young people must somehow reassert our authority—and I am not ashamed to use what Max Beloff calls 'one of the most emotive "boo-words" of the moment'—to insist on standards from those who are dependent on us and on society, and also our belief that those should be the fundamental standards of simple goodness, not the debased standards which adult society too often allows itself. We as adults have the task of civilizing and socializing the young who, when we first get our hands on them, are after all nothing more than small animals. If they grow up into nothing better than large animals—and the human animal can be the nastiest, dirtiest, cruellest and most dangerous animal in creation—then it is we who have fallen down on the job. A great deal is wrong with some young people and I am very much afraid that it is too late for them. We have already spoiled them or allowed others to do so and ours is a heavy burden of responsibility. But every minute of every day, new young lives are born into this world which we have made for them, and it is not too late to see that they do not go the same way as Angela of London or Alison of Kent, Ohio. For let us never forget the Chinese proverb which says that it is one generation that opens up the road which the next generation travels.

First and foremost, nations such as Britain and the United States have got to face fairly and squarely the problems of the slums in which too many of our children are growing up, slums which are, as they have ever been, the breeding-ground for every kind of delinquency, from vandalism to out-and-out criminal activities. How can anyone expect a boy to be anything but antisocial towards a society that allows him to live in one room in a derelict house condemned ten years ago, with leaking roof and boarded-up windows? What chance has a girl of twelve who has to stay off school twice a week in order to look after two younger children while her mother visits her father in prison? (Do we think sufficiently about who are the real sufferers when a husband and father goes to prison?)

It may be argued that slums are no worse today than they ever were so they cannot be the cause of present-day troubles. I think there is an obvious answer to that, and it lies in the increasing mobility of the population. In the old days children and young people in the slums rarely ventured beyond the end of their street and had little or no idea of how the other half lived. Nowadays, although wages may be inadequate when it comes to buying a house, most families try somehow or other to have a television set, and the affluence of the world comes right into the cold, dirty room. So does its violence and greed; and the deprived children, as soon as they are old enough to travel any distance, venture out to loot and destroy in inarticulate protest and fury at a world which condemns them at birth to intolerable conditions, whether in a London slum or in a New York ghetto. Along with slum homes, they have slum schools, many of them built before the turn of the century, dark, dismal erections with outside lavatories and an asphalt yard the only playground. None but the most dedicated of teachers will go and teach there, and many even of those cannot stand the conditions and leave after a short time, so that the turnover of staff is high and the children are inadequately taught and deprived of any stable relationships. There are schools where almost every child is on probation, where every day someone is off school attending the juvenile court. It is a vicious circle: teachers do not want to teach in such schools, but, unless teachers are forthcoming, the state of the children gets worse.

Needless to say, these children are the virtual write-offs of the educational system. Despite the peculiar theories of Michael Duane, I cannot subscribe to the idea that all children have equal intelligence and it is only their environment which determines their success or failure. I believe that it is probably true that *most* slum-dwellers are of fairly limited intelligence. If it were not so, they would have somehow fought their way out of the slums. It is not their fault but it is a fact of life, and although unintelligent parents sometimes have surprisingly intelligent children, it is more usual for their children to take after them. They are born into this highly competitive rat-race of a technological world with the disability of below-average intelligence and a background almost completely devoid of any kind of culture.

Yet these are the children with the worst schools and the least adequate teaching. In a selective system of education, they would not stand a cat in hell's chance of a grammar school, not only because of poor teaching but also because of their own truancy, for they feel no incentive to attend school regularly and in these areas, welfare and attendance officers cannot cope. Neither is the comprehensive system likely to do them much good, for it is almost certainly going to be some botched-up scheme of linked schools in the same old buildings (and with the same old teachers or rather lack of them) as before. In fact, the occasional clever child from the slums will, in my opinion, lose what chances he had under the old system. If by a miracle he scraped a grammar-school place, this took him out of the ghetto into a world of different standards, where he sat at the next desk to a boy from a suburban home and found him a likeable human being and not, as he might have imagined, a 'stuck-up snob'. I am far from confident that, in the neighbourhood comprehensive school, probably composed of two secondary moderns several miles from each other, where his friends are the boys from the same back streets as his own, the rare clever child will even be noticed by those birds of passage who are his teachers.

It is these deprived children, fatally handicapped by their homes and environment, for whom our educational system makes little or no provision. They are the slow learners who, if not identified at an early age (where are the nursery schools for these children?) and given immediate help, will only learn that school and failure are one and the same thing. Recent statistics have shown some twelve per cent of children to be 'in distress', and it is likely that twenty per cent are slow learners to some degree. These children know the misery of unimportance and express it in the only way open to them: in violence, vandalism and rebellion. Sir Alec Clegg, chief education officer of the West Riding of Yorkshire, said at the official celebrations of the centenary of the 1870 Education Act: 'Secondary education for all must be what adult society wills it to be, and if the only challenge we can offer the young is that of material prosperity, and we overvalue the quick who can add to it and discard the slow who cannot, the former will despise our values and the latter resent our indifference. We shall blame both for what is our failing and there will be much bitterness and much discord in our society.'

At the same time, Dr Kathleen Ollerenshaw, chairman of Manchester Education Committee, warned that unless money was forthcoming on a scale far outstripping present expenditure on education, standards would have to be drastically *reduced*, and that Government and local authorities would have a heavy bill to pay. It is nothing to the bill that we shall all have to pay in human misery if we do not undertake a massive programme of tearing down the bug-ridden slum houses and the rat-ridden slum schools and so take away from our children two of the main causes of their delinquency. Economic crisis or not, we are a rich nation and we must not—we *dare* not—tolerate the slums any longer.

163

But what is the use of my writing this? People have been say-ing it for years and still nothing is done, either here or in America, the richest country in the world, but with some of the most horrifying poverty and social inequalities. Money, money and more money is needed, and as a nation we need to get our priorities right. So long as we are selfish, stupid and greedy enough to spend infinitely more on gambling, tobacco and alcohol than we spend on the education of our children, we have only ourselves to blame for the evils which have befallen us; but it is a pity that the sins of the fathers have to be visited on the children.

This then is what the whole of society must be prepared to do if we are to halt the crime, the vandalism, the violence which we see in the young and which show every sign of intensifying and increasing throughout our whole way of life. I am not so starry-eyed as to imagine, as some early socialists did, that all you needed to do to create utopia was to put people into council houses with gardens, but it is at least a start. Let us have a Government, of whatever persuasion, big enough to get its mind off vote-catching and scoring off the Opposition, which will tell the nation the truth: that it has *got* to produce the money to carry out this gigantic task or else face an unimaginable future.

Let us pretend for one blissful moment that we have got our schools. What then are we going to do with the children in them in order to educate them for commitment and responsibility? In fact, we do not need to imagine all those new schools for we dare not wait for them. What should we be doing *now* in the schools which we already have? I am all too well aware that the ideals which many schools strive for are impossible because of the handicaps already mentioned: bad buildings and shortage of staff. We all know that there have been examples of saintly souls in crippled bodies, and quite often a school can surmount most magnificently the obstacles of lack of space and beauty. But this, like saintliness, is unusual, and it is not true that buildings make no difference. Many schools are facing impos-sible odds and it is difficult to know what help anyone can give them.

I heard recently of a London school which had been forced

into a makeshift comprehensive system and which had had three headmistresses in eight years, and even more deputy heads. What had been a reasonably good secondary modern school was now a shockingly bad so-called comprehensive school, with staff leaving in droves and delinquency rising at an alarming rate. One thing which can be done for difficult schools in out-of-date buildings and deprived areas is not to force through by Act of Parliament and against the better judgement of local authority and teachers completely unworkable schemes of secondary reorganization.

I believe that the worst thing that can happen to a child is not to count—not to matter. Indeed, it is surely the worst thing that can happen to any human being, child or adult. A very great deal of the trouble in the Western world today springs from this basic feeling of complete insignificance and impotence which has been growing up amongst us for many years and never faster than in the past decade. The over-riding purpose of education nowadays should be to establish the importance of the individual, even in this machine-dominated, overgoverned society. Everybody should matter, and this principle must be established at the earliest possible stage of a child's schooling.

The great criticism of the tripartite system of education and selection at eleven plus is that it rejects as second-class citizens eighty per cent of the child population. I do not happen to believe that this rejection is inherent in the selection procedure, but it is largely the result of the subversive activities of those who, almost as soon as the Butler Act was on the statute-book, began to denigrate the newly established secondary modern schools. Instead of being given a fair chance (and ample resources) wherewith to achieve the parity of esteem which was supposed to be their right, these schools were constantly told by members of the educational Left that they were vastly inferior to the grammar schools, that their pupils were rejects, failures at eleven, and fit only to become hewers of wood and drawers of water. One must assume that these misguided people were sincere, that they were genuinely concerned for the non-grammar school pupils and that they seriously believed that only by arousing the resentment of the majority of parents, the parents of the secondary modern children, against the grammar schools and by demonstrating the awful inferiority of the schools to which their children had been 'condemned', would they be able to destroy the hated middle-class 'snob-schools' (as they called the grammar schools) and set up their classical ideal of comprehensives for all.

What never seemed to occur to them was that, in painting this depressing picture of neurotic children almost driven to suicide by failure at eleven and the relegation to the scrap-heap of secondary modern school, they were doing a serious injury to the children whom they most wished to help. You cannot tell generations of children and their parents for thirty years that they are failures and of no account without the message finally getting through. It was *not* the system that rejected the non-academic children, it was the critics of the system who told them constantly that they *were* rejected. The voices of the thousands of dedicated teachers in first-rate secondary modern schools, raised in protest against the abuse and scorn poured on their schools and their efforts within those schools, went unheard and unheeded. Thanks to the stupidity of the pro-comprehensivists, who were prepared to use any stick to beat the selection dog, 'secondary modern child' became synonymous with failure, throw-out, reject, worthless. Not all the purpose-built comprehensives in the world will now undo the harm done to children by these blind fools.

I am *not* arguing in favour of selection nor making a plea for the retention of the grammar schools: that is beyond the scope of this book. What I am doing is pointing out that, as in so many things that have been done in the sacred name of egalitarianism, the very last thing that has been considered by its fanatical supporters is the children in the schools.

It will be a long time before this feeling of inferiority, induced in the non-academic child by those who set themselves up as his champions, will disappear. In fact, if the large comprehensives become dominated with a desire for academic honours and if all the responsible jobs in the schools go to the academic seniors, as may easily happen, the last state of the 'Newsom child' may very well be worse than the first. Just as a feeling of inferiority has been bred into generations of secondary modern schoolchildren since the attack on these schools began in the Forties, so it may well be that the unpleasant arrogance which we are now seeing in some of the products of the grammar schools, and which is a relatively recent phenomenon, is a result of being told that they are the *crème de la crème*, the selected few who are being given the best of everything, even at the expense of all the rest of their age-group. It is not going to be easy for the schools to undo all the harm that has been done, not—and let me emphasize this— by the selective system itself but by those critics who, in seeking to destroy it, either created or else made very much worse the attitudes of mind which they claimed to deplore.

It looks as though the majority of the schools in the Seventies are going to be comprehensive schools, whether we like it or not. Let there be no mistake about it, very large numbers of people in this country do not like it but, as in so many ways nowadays when individual choice seems to count for less and less, they are going to have to lump it. The teachers in these schools are going to need every ounce of judgement and discrimination if they are to achieve greater flexibility and freedom without sacrificing what is of proved and permanent value. I am very much afraid that at least some of the rootlessness and restlessness of youth springs from the chaos which has been caused in some schools by over-hasty and bad schemes of reorganization. Far too much has been done for the sake of mere administrative convenience— the establishment of one large co-educational school, for example, in the place of two smaller single-sex schools, regardless of the wishes of the parents and the children and of whether smaller and more homogeneous units might not have provided better opportunities for educational nurture.

I should like to quote from a speech made in 1966 by Sir Alec Clegg, as great a champion then of the underprivileged child as he is today and a heart-and-soul comprehensivist. He said at a conference of headmistresses at which I was present:

> The real dangers which those of us who believe in comprehensive schools have to tackle are those which arise from the convictions of our friends who think that all our educational problems will be

solved by this organizational change, whereas some of the most grievous problems of our day may be unaffected or even aggravated by it. Take for example our lack of understanding of the education of the slow learner. I am quite convinced myself that this is our major problem. Will this inevitably be helped by comprehensive education? Indeed if the ingredients of success are more compassion, more individual understanding and a greater aspiration, a child may well be worse off, not better, in a large comprehensive school. The same applies to the distressed child, who could more easily pass unnoticed in a large community than a small. I do not say for a moment that this need be so, but it will be so in an insensitive school, and a large insensitive school is a more dangerous institution than a small insensitive school. The discarding of the less intellectual child—this *can* happen in a comprehensive school as much as in any other school.

He concluded his address with these words:

If massive comprehensive schools dominated by one university admission examination is to be the pattern of our future education system, all I can say is heaven help the education of this country. If we are to go forward with this immense change in our system, as I think we should, we must guard against improvisations which may be organizationally sound but educationally harmful, and above all we must face squarely the dangers of comprehensive education and acknowledge its limitations.

I do not know whether those who are hell-bent on forcing comprehensiveness through at all costs have ever heard or read that warning but they would do well to heed it, for, serious though the problems are that we have now with the young, they are nothing to what we shall have in the future if Sir Alec's prophecies come true. Children from bad, unhappy or deprived homes, children with personality problems, with problems of learning, do not suddenly shed all these disadvantages when lumped together in a two-thousand-strong school, no matter how much gleaming glass and shining concrete have gone into its building nor how much expensive hardware there is in its specialist rooms. All that happens is that the number of children with problems in any school is doubled, trebled, even quadrupled and, as any teacher knows, two problem children are not just twice as difficult as one, they are four times as difficult.

However, having taken due heed of the warning that we need not expect miracles from comprehensive schools and, indeed, that some of the ills which they are intended to remedy may actually be intensified by them, what should we be teaching our children if we are to rescue them from their twin enemies of insignificance and boredom, from which, I am sure, springs so much of their rebellion? We hear a lot about participation today although not very much is done about it. In our schools, a very great deal should be done about it and, in many schools, is being done. Although the head cannot abdicate from the responsibility of making final decisions, since he and he alone is accountable, nevertheless every effort must be made to make the school something approaching a participant democracy. I am not going to go into all the different ways of doing this for there are so many, depending on the administrative set-up of the school, but they can range from a simple suggestion-box through form periods, the house system, year tutors to a full-blown school council, all of them with freedom to discuss and criticize practically every aspect of school life. There is no better way of helping young people to understand the principles of democracy and also the need to accept certain authority within the democratic system, than through listening, discussing, explaining why some of their suggestions are practical and others quite impossible. At all levels in our schools, we must be constantly helping our children to realize that they are important to the community and can be actively involved in its life.

There are two dangers to be guarded against in setting up this kind of living democracy in a school. First, we must never make the mistake of thinking that children and young people want the sort of phony democracy practised in a few very small and very progressive (sic) schools, where there is no authority at all and everyone does exactly as he likes. A friend of mine teaches in a very conventional grammar school where the pupils wear uniform, call the masters 'sir', get up when a mistress comes into a room and open the door for her when she goes out. A party of boys from a very progressive school visited this citadel of old-fashioned tradition. When the grammar-school staff were told that the visitors might expect to call them by their Christian names, one senior master was heard to say darkly that anyone calling *him* by his first name would get a 'thick ear'. Perhaps this warning was duly conveyed to the visitors for, in the event, they had only been at the school a few days before *they* were saying 'sir', opening doors, etcetera. There was also a marked improvement in their personal appearance! Just before they left, one of them remarked wistfully that he rather liked it there. *You knew where you were.*

The second danger to avoid is creating so much participation that the children are wearied by time-consuming committees and all the rest of the paraphernalia of democracy in action. It is a good thing for them to realize that, if they wish to have a voice in shaping their own futures, then they must be prepared to spend time on rather tedious details and that nothing but trouble can come from leaving the busybodies to do everything, but at the same time a tactful adult needs to be present to see that councils, committees and so on do not degenerate into mere talking-shops with nothing getting done at all.

In a book of this sort, I obviously cannot discuss at length matters of curriculum and teaching methods. These would only be of interest to practising teachers, to whom I would not in any case presume to dictate. The one essential thing which must lie at the root of everything we do in the schools, whether in what we teach or in the way the school is organized, is this business of letting the individual child know that he matters, that no one is second-rate and useless and that everyone can produce something worth while, be it a neatly typed business letter or a well-risen sponge cake, a piece of sculpture or a Latin prose. What is important is that children should be led to appreciate and admire achievement and talent, of no matter what kind, however greater than or different from their own it may be. Apart from the educationally subnormal, with whom we are not dealing, there is no child alive who cannot do *something* reasonably well, something which in the doing will give him pride, self-confidence and a degree of happiness. Whatever else the school does with him, it must discover what that something is and encourage him to do it to the very best of his ability. The primary concern of the schools should be, in the words of the Crowther Report, not the living the children will earn but the life they will lead. If we are turning out from our schools a whole generation of boys and girls who are so bored that they have to turn to drugs or violence for kicks, then we are failing them.

One aspect of school life on which infinitely more money will have to be spent if we are to prepare our children for the increased leisure which undoubtedly is one of the causes of boredom and its attendant evils, is what are usually known as 'extra-curricular activities'. There may be very little that education can do to lessen the boredom of repetitive machine-minding work, but it should be possible for us so to furnish the minds of the young people going into these jobs that they will accept with a degree of cheerfulness the necessity for them in a modern community. They will only do this if they have been taught how to use their leisure in more rewarding ways than bingo, the telly, the dance-hall and coffee-bar.

It may seem an absolute pipe-dream to talk about the provision on a generous scale of residential courses for children, but this is one of the things which must be done. No Government which cares about children should talk about putting the screws on the public schools, as a Minister of Education did recently. Quite apart from the fact that I find it profoundly shocking that an ex-headmaster should use the language of the medieval torture chamber in connection with anything that has to do with children, it should be the policy of every party to *increase* the provision of boarding-schools, not drive out of business those that already exist. Every child should have the opportunity to spend considerable periods in his school life in a residential community, learning a greater sense of responsibility towards other people and being introduced to constructive and worth-while leisure pursuits.

When I first went to work in Manchester, it came as a shock to me to discover, when working on the English panel of the committee setting the eleven-plus examination, that one had to avoid any essay question which assumed that the children would have visited either the seaside or the country. This is a city a short bus-run from some of the loveliest scenery in the British Isles and only forty miles from the sea. It seemed impossible in the affluent society, but it was a fact vouched for by all of my primary-school colleagues.

There needs to be a complete change of outlook on the part of the people and Government of this country as to what they mean to make of their boys and girls. At present, a very great deal of the really important work of a school is done by a few dedicated teachers in their spare time, and this is rightly known as 'out-of-school activities'. Children cannot be obliged to stay after four o'clock for drama, music, athletics; and it is all too often the very child who is most in need of what the school clubs can give him who is 'unclubbable'. Either that or he (more probably she) has to go home quickly to look after younger children or get father's tea ready. As for being able to go off to the school camp or join the trip abroad in the holidays, that is out of the question. Canoeing, mountaineering, sailing, riding, are all denied to the children who most need to develop physical activities since they are less able to find meaningful intellectual activities. How are our children to know anything at all about the quality of life if their horizons are never widened beyond the streets of their own city?

If education is intended to prepare a child to cope with living, then we have to see that he can face the challenge of this technological age and play his part in producing wealth so that he and the rest of the community to which he will be happy to belong may enjoy 'the good life'. And this is a very different thing from merely having a good time, the sterile ambition of the eternally bored.

School then must help a child to see the value of work as something to be enjoyed and to take a pride in, and at the same time it must prepare him to use his leisure creatively, both for himself and for the benefit of others, but above all it must help him to realize himself as an individual.

The more one thinks about this problem, the more apparent it becomes that it is the impersonality of modern life which lies at the root of many of our troubles. It is so easy to become convinced that one does not matter and, after that, that nothing matters at all. America is probably the most automated and 'depersonalized' place I know, if I may be allowed that rather dreadful word. It is also the country where one is constantly being offered 'your own personalized' this, that and the other, as though there were a desperate need—as indeed there is—to assure you that you do still exist as a separate, personal entity. So everything we do in our schools must be permeated with our intention to educate our children to see themselves as individuals and as members of society, with a twin responsibility to themselves and to others. They must grow up to be whole people, coming to terms with the real world, imperfect and fraught with trouble and difficulties though it may be, rather than dropping out into an unreal world of Maoist slogans, utopian dreams or drug-induced fantasies.

12

Sin Makes History

A complete change of temper and outlook on the part of the people of this country. What exactly does this imply, apart from a willingness to spend a very great deal more on education than we have done up to now?

Some little while ago, in the House of Commons, a Conservative member called attention to the problems of the permissive society and moved:

> That this House views with grave concern the continuing decline of moral standards and the increases of violence, hooliganism, drug-taking and obscenity and the consequent undermining of family life; and calls upon Her Majesty's Government to enlist the support of parents, religious leaders, school and university teachers, broadcasters and social workers to give help to those members of the rising generation who may be in need of adequate discipline and a better example.

I am probably politically naïve but I have read his speech with some care and nowhere can I read into it an attack, either overt or concealed, on the Labour Government of the day. Yet the ensuing debate degenerated into yet another unseemly wrangle on party lines, with Labour members hotly denying that there was *any* deterioration in moral standards because, they alleged, the Conservatives were trying to blame them for this deterioration. Instead of a serious discussion about a serious matter which certainly causes much concern to ordinary people, certain Members seemed to treat it very lightly, making silly jokes and hurling childish insults across the floor of the House, and so we were treated to the same old spectacle of the parties lining up on opposite sides, whereas if ever there was an issue on which all men of good-will should be on the same side, this was surely it.

Equally frivolous and unworthy of a great newspaper was the comment in *The Times* on the debate. The reporter appeared to

174

find the whole debate very amusing, with all these square old fuddy-duddies sounding off about immorality, as if anyone cared! For half a column, he jeered at members of both parties, using such phrases as 'mighty sermons', 'the unsullied heights of St Marylebone', 'a saintly halo', and so on, making it absolutely clear to his readers that he agreed whole-heartedly with Dr Robinson when he called the permissive society 'a step toward maturity'.

I would certainly not agree with the bishop, who, in my opinion, has done his church and society in general no little harm by this and other 'liberal' pronouncements. On the other hand, I would equally not subscribe to the opinion of one writer who points to what he calls an appalling record 'of the most morally reprehensible legislation ever passed in so short a space of time by any Government we have record of in history'. Nevertheless, I feel that he may have put his finger on something of importance with the words 'in so short a space of time'. Although each of the Acts of Parliament to which this writer objects (he mentions betting, homosexuality, abortion and divorce) was introduced out of genuine concern for people or even out of a desire to help the police or the medical profession, the cumulative effect of so much permissive legislation *in little more than five years* has been unhelpful to the young. I cannot think that I would have voted against any one of these measures had I been in Parliament, yet I do not feel that there should have been such urgency to rush them all through (except for the Betting Act, which was introduced by an earlier Government) in the life of one Parliament, and almost certainly against the wishes of large sections of the population. Opinion-polls are not, as we have seen, infallible but they made it pretty clear that on each of these issues, the majority of people were actually opposed to the legislation passed in their name. There had certainly been nothing in the election manifesto of either party which gave Parliament a mandate for so much controversial legislation.

If the motion before the House deploring permissiveness really was just a gimmick, it is a great pity. If it was not, it is even more of a pity that M.P.s of all parties did not rise to the occasion and support it. Several references were made in the debate to the innate decency of the British public, 'essentially extraordinary respectable people', according to one M.P. I absolutely agree with this finding, but it is these respectable people who are puzzled and disturbed at many of the things mentioned by the proposer of the original motion: the dissolution of many traditions, the decline in religious and moral standards in society, the rise in the illegitimacy rate and in divorce, in crime (especially violent crime) and in hooliganism, the continued use of four-letter words and gross sexual antics on the stage. Like the member for Wellingborough, they feel that taste has reached an exceedingly low level when a leading figure in the National Theatre takes it upon himself to be responsible for the production of *Oh! Calcutta!* Despairing of getting any guidance from the church, these people look to their leaders in Parliament, and what do they get? An entirely superficial treatment of the question and a level of debate hardly worthy of a preparatory school. They look in vain for men of genuine principle and integrity, men prepared to admit that they may have made a mistake and that the consequences of so much permissive legislation in so short a time have not been wholly good. Obviously, there can be no question of repealing laws already on the statute-book, nor would I personally want such a thing to happen, but I do believe that it would help the millions of people who are beginning to lose faith in decency and to think that they are 'old-fashioned' and prudish in deploring much that is happening around them if some of our leaders would actually do some leading for a change instead of riding the permissive band-wagon with the rest of the frightened people.

I do not think that I am alone in failing to see the necessity of the Latey Committee and in thinking its findings misguided and not in the best interests of young people. Unless giving the vote to the teenagers was a mere matter of grabbing a few more votes for the Left, as has been suggested to me by quite a number of young people of all political persuasions, I can see no point whatsoever in lowering the age of majority. Nor, as far as I can see, can the majority of eighteen-year-olds. All this silly piece of sycophantic vote-catching has done is to inflate the already oversized ego of the least responsible section of the young.

Since the new law came into being we have celebrated—if that is the word for such maimed rites—several coming-of-age birthdays at my school. The girls felt the whole thing to be farcical, for what, they said, was the point of being called adult when you had not yet got out of school uniform, still had your 'A' levels to face and would be financially dependent on someone, be it Father or the tax-payer, for at least another three years. Even those young people who leave school at fifteen (and it will soon be sixteen) cannot possibly have had sufficient experience of what it means to be a part of the adult community with adult commitments and responsibilities by the time they are eighteen, and it is utterly ridiculous to have given adult status to boys and girls still at school.

An extraordinary amount of nonsense is talked about earlier maturity, as though children were *immeasurably* more mature physically than their counterparts were ten, twenty, even fifty years ago. This simply is not true: statistics are produced which purport to show that girls menstruate one year earlier than they did one hundred years ago, but what in the world has that got to do with their fitness to vote at eighteen? When I look back to my own schooldays I can remember perfectly well when I and all my friends reached the exciting age when we could call ourselves women, and, believe me, we were still little girls!

As far as I can see—and I have had first-hand knowledge of this matter for forty years—there has been practically no difference in the age at which girls reach maturity over those years, especially since no two girls are alike. One can look at a class of fourteen-year-olds and realize that many of them are physically very mature whereas many are still undeveloped with no more 'figure' than a little boy.

To take this spurious argument of earlier physical maturity as an excuse for lowering the age of majority has merely made yet another contribution to the social ills of the Seventies. At a time when a sizeable proportion of the young are showing themselves to be almost completely devoid of responsibility, culture, taste, manners and morals, it is mad to give them more power than they already have. As for students who, from their intolerance, violence and obscenity, would not have been out of place in Nazi Germany, not only are they not fit to exercise adult responsibilities now but one wonders whether they ever will be. It is a thousand pities that any Government should have sought the easy popularity of permissiveness, with M.B.E.s to pop singers and votes at eighteen, when the country was asking for a clear lead in re-establishing some kind of restraint on the worst excesses of the young.

Dr Bryan Wilson in his essay on the age of majority has suggested that, instead of giving more power to the teenagers, a responsible Government would be seeking means to curb the 'live-now-pay-later' philosophy of the youth culture in the interests of everyone except those who batten on youth. Though it is probably too much to expect of the new Government that it should now take away the privileges given to youth, however mistaken its predecessors may have been to give such privileges in the first place, the nation has every right to ask its leaders to call a halt, at least for the time being, to permissive legislation and to anything which tends to strengthen the hands of the young against their elders.

If it is true that the great majority of people, both young and old, would welcome a clear-cut denunciation from their leaders of the corrupting influences which are making life intolerable for some of the old and leading too many of the young to disease and an early death, would it then be possible to reverse the trend towards corruption?

Many will say that it is not possible, that one cannot put the clock back, but the lessons of history would seem to disprove this. Man has never made steady progress, for his story is one of peaks and troughs, of pendulum swings between periods of licence and periods of puritanism. All too often the licence has led to decadence and the virtual destruction of civilization. The difference between our situation now and that of man in earlier crises is that in the second half of the twentieth century and in a democratic society man should not only be able to recognize and isolate the destructive virus but also be able to render it harmless, even destroy it.

Many of those who dislike the permissive society comfort themselves with the thought that there will inevitably be a tremendous swing back to authoritarianism and puritan morality. If this were to happen—though it is much more likely that Western civilization will succumb to decadence and be for the second time overrun by the barbarians—then I for one would deplore it. If we are to escape both these fates, one only slightly more nasty than the other, then society has got to make a positive effort to rid itself of the cancer which is slowly but surely undermining its health.

The whole of the entertainment industry needs to be cleaned up, from the sedulous anti-culture of *Top of the Pops* to the pornographic films and books which disgrace our cities. Reputable newspapers should ask themselves whether they really approve of critics who hail obscenity on stage, film and in print as a courageous breakthrough in art, just as publishers and theatre-managers need to consider their true motives in encouraging public mutilation of the values which constitute our well-being, happiness and personal security.

It is the entertainment industry more than any other which has created the pernicious youth cult, and it has only done it with one aim in mind—money. If there is an unholy trinity which should take most of the blame for the corruption of the young, it is television, radio and the gramophone-record industry, for it is they who have sponsored the rotten 'heroes' of the pop-culture with their phony philosophies based on drugs, sex and violence. If I believed in the medieval hell, I would reserve a special section of particular nastiness for the evil men who, in order to line their pockets with the money taken from the teenagers, have given them as their idols Mick Jagger and John Lennon.

Of course, as soon as anyone dares to mention any form of censorship in connection with what passes for art (although where art comes into it when one is dealing with ninety-nine per cent of the pop world I would not really know) there is a howl from the progressives about interference with the freedom of the individual. I cannot see that this argument holds water at all. If we make laws about the consumption of alcohol and dangerous drugs, if we prohibit T.V. advertisements for cigarettes, if we prevent people from committing acts of indecency in public, I can see absolutely no reason why we should allow subtler forms of corruption. If for instance the B.B.C. and I.T.V. will not face their responsibilities, then I have no hesitation whatsoever in saying that they must be obliged to do so, since it is obviously the will of most of the people in this country that they stop brainwashing the viewers into acceptance of debased standards of morality. There is no reason at all that I can see why a Government which can forbid the advertising of cigarettes on T.V. cannot forbid the selling of sex and violence, both in advertisements and in so-called entertainment.

I do not care how many critics howl me down and call me a kill-joy for saying this. If the only joy they can find in life consists in watching scenes of lust and murder and listening to profanity, blasphemy and smutty innuendo, then I am sorry for them, but I am still sorrier for the children who will be swept to destruction on the tide of filth emanating from these debased minds if the present trend is not halted. It is idle to pretend that people are not influenced by what they see. If this were true, why should commercial firms spend millions on advertising, especially on television? American television was recently accused by a presidential commission of serving civilization 'in an appalling way'. If millions of people can be persuaded to buy washing-powders, cat-food, soft drinks, chocolates and a host of other things, if they are even assumed to be vulnerable to the sweet-talk of party political broadcasts, no one can pretend that they remain totally unaffected by the less direct message of the medium. One assumes that both B.B.C. and I.T.V. are responsible to *someone* in authority. Can that someone not take his courage in both hands and at the risk of being called square tell the beardies and weirdies who seem to use the medium largely for their own satisfaction that the public has had enough?

'Sin makes history, goodness is silent,' said Goethe. Whether or not it is true that sin makes history, it certainly makes news, and never more than in the last decade or so. Earlier in this book I asked whether we might not call a moratorium on the publicizing of sex. If the young who have lost their bearings are ever to find their way back to the right road, then I suggest that we also need a moratorium on the publicizing of the views and actions of the dissident minority, and of the worthless and dangerous people whose lightest word and most trivial action have to be trumpeted to the world by the mass media, merely because they are 'personalities'.

The evil of making semi-heroic figures out of the train robbers is obvious, but the public will always be fascinated by crime on so grand a scale as this and one can make allowances. What I completely fail to understand is why any reputable newspaper wasted money sending reporters and cameramen to interview John Lennon and his wife in their ridiculous 'love-in', or whatever they called it. Personally, if they had both retired into their bag and never emerged again, I and the great mass of humanity could not have cared less; yet there they were, day after day, in the newspapers and on T.V., with reporters solemnly copying down every bit of nonsense that fell from their lips and faithfully relaying it to the public. Of all the babies which are born into the world every day, the only ones we hear about (apart from the newsworthy multiple births) are the illegitimate offspring (or else the terminated pregnancies) of the mistresses of pop stars, film-directors and other admirable models for the young to follow! If consenting adults want to live together and produce children without benefit of clergy, that is entirely their own affair and I have not the slightest interest in preventing them, but I would not choose to parade their eccentric behaviour before the young and immature, thus giving the impression that adultery and illegitimacy are the norm rather than the exception and, since they are indulged in by their heroes and heroines, highly admirable behaviour.

Going back as far as 1967, it was a less than happy choice of the B.B.C. to make Sandie Shaw, still in her teens, Britain's representative in the Eurovision song contest the week after she had been co-respondent in a particularly unsavoury divorce. The very day that she had been severely reprimanded by the judge for wrecking a marriage, her picture adorned the cover of the *Radio Times*, giving impressionable teenagers the clear message that the judge was an old square and that the State-subsidized B.B.C. accepted teenage adultery and marriage-wrecking as O.K. behaviour.

It would make a refreshing change if Press, radio and T.V. commentators as well as psychologists and sociologists would assume now and again that there are some young people who are not anarchists, sexually promiscuous, or addicted to drugs, and that there is nothing particularly square about normality. Only recently I heard a reference on the radio to a survey which had been done of the sex life of women undergraduates. In the first place, I feel that the researcher might have found something better to do than to pester young women between the ages of eighteen and twenty-one into telling him whether or not they were on the Pill. I cannot see what possible use such a survey can be to anyone at all, except for giving the researcher the excuse to ask impertinent questions. Whatever he may have expected to find, one got the distinct impression from the radio report that he had been surprised, if not a little disappointed, at finding that a very large percentage of the girls interviewed had not had intercourse. One phrase used of these decent young women was illuminating: they were referred to as 'sexually retarded'. I think I have rarely heard a more irresponsible comment.

The antics of the mass media in publicizing every trivial act or word of the young merely because they *are* young are so pathetic that I have often thought what bliss it would be if for six months all news of the under-twenties could be banned. I am prepared to bet that there would be an abrupt end of their futile demonstrations if the cameras and reporters were not there to glorify them. Going to demos has become an entertaining way of spending the weekend for some undergraduates. I am told that a list goes up on the Union notice-board and they peruse it to see what is going on that looks like providing a bit of excitement. It is certainly a fact that the same old faces are seen at every protest march or sit-in, and these are not only the professional agitators but the idle publicity-seekers who have nothing better to do with their time and money than traipse from one university to another. At a recent sit in at a Scottish university, when the occupiers of the buildings were rounded up, only two or three were actually students of the university, the rest coming from far and wide, many of them not students of anything at all. If no one gave advance publicity to these demos, if *no* adults went anywhere near the sites except for the minimum of police needed to check destructive tendencies, if there was no sign of a T.V. camera and no word in the next day's papers, in short, if the adult world completely ignored the whole silly business, then most of the fun would be taken out of their antics. What is utterly deplorable is the encouragement given this useless form of dissent by those Peter Pans of protest who don their self-consciously proletarian gear and go marching with the young. Unfortunately, the chief offenders are often clergy, almost invariably those with a T.V. image to uphold—so open-minded that all their convictions have run out!

If any of the young whose opinions are sought so eagerly by Press and television had anything of interest to say, one could understand the publicity given to them, but almost invariably the poor dears talk the most terrible nonsense. What, for instance, is one to make of the undergraduate who sought to excuse the howling-down of the Labour Foreign Secretary at the Oxford Union debate on the grounds that 'we all knew what Mr Stewart was going to say'? One is reminded of the girl who did not want to be given a book for her birthday because she already had one, and would not go to a performance of *Hamlet* because she knew the ending! Absolutely typical of the sort of empty and meaningless rhetoric which is all one gets from many of the much-publicized spokesmen of the young was the battle-cry of Joan Baez at the Washington anti-Cambodian-invasion demo. If I recall her aright, her closing words were: 'We have to be *free*! Free to do what we have to do!' What an anticlimax! Because at no point had she given the slightest clue as to what it actually was that she or they or anyone else *had* to do.

I have already commented on the dreary platitudes spouted by the famous gathering of student rebels from all over Europe. A similar 'confrontation', to use the latest in-word, occurred just after the age of majority had been lowered. With great publicity in the *Radio Times*, we were presented with a representative (?) gathering of eighteen-year-olds who proceeded to talk the hind leg off a donkey for an hour and say absolutely nothing. According to the *Radio Times*, some of the youngsters were relatively 'normal'—a nurse, an apprentice, even a young soldier. Needless to say, we were not even told who they were, much less given the chance to listen to them. Once again, we had to endure discontented sixth-formers and first-year undergraduates telling us how they would reorganize the schools and universities—at least, *not* telling us, because clearly they did not know how. All that emerged from their turgid arguments was that they advocated perpetual change as an excellent thing. As one sixth-former said, 'We want everything to be in a state of flux all the time.' The two adults who had unsuspectingly allowed themselves to be lured on to the same programme very soon gave up trying to interrupt the flow of earnest inanities and sat back in silence, looking uncomfortable.

True to form, when the first eighteen-year-old cast her vote in a by-election, every national paper plus the B.B.C. and I.T.V. were there to record and film her words of wisdom, which were so completely unmemorable that I have forgotten what they were, but I remember wondering at the time whether the reporters' journeys were really necessary. Just after Mick Jagger went to Australia, there appeared in most newspapers long accounts of an interview which he had given. Now, I would have thought that the only subject on which this young man is competent to speak is pop music, and, though I do not like his music and heartily dislike what I know of his personality, I am prepared to take note of his views on matters on which he has some expertise. To my surprise, although I suppose it was naïve of me still to be surprised at anything the mass-media do in respect of the heroes of the youth cult, he was not asked by the reporters to comment on music. Instead, he gave his views on marriage and children, on which subjects I should hardly have thought him an expert. More was to come: after dismissing the married state and the family in a few ill-chosen words, he was next invited to give to a waiting world his views on God and religion, about which topics he knew even less than he did about marriage and parenthood. I really wish that I could have got inside the mind of the interviewer who seriously considered that Mick Jagger was a fit and proper person to pontificate for the benefit of millions of readers on some of the most serious and important issues that man faces in his life.

Another of the great non-events of the contemporary scene, which perfectly illustrates everything that I most dislike in the adulation of the young, is the rise to fame of Bernadette Devlin. I do not think that I have ever listened to anyone, not even among the young, who talks so much and says so little as that grossly over-rated and over-publicized young woman. She is the almost classical example of the ineffectualness of the young when suddenly given the power, the participation, for which they are constantly screaming. By means of a glib tongue and belliger-ence she has exploited the bitterness of her people and has persuaded them to send her—*twice*—to Westminster, having done nothing but add fuel to the flames of an already explosive situation. The reception she was given in Parliament was nauseating, there is no other word. Merely because she was young, and a woman into the bargain—although the violence of her language and actions did little credit to her sex—almost without exception M.P.s fawned upon her and positively drooled over her. To do her justice, she probably found their flattery as sickeningly fulsome as I did. As for the Press and T.V., they really outdid themselves. The foreign Press reception given for her at the Dorchester sticks in my mind. There she was like a prima donna with hard-bitten pressmen crowding round, scribbling every word as if she were Joan of Arc telling the inside story of the siege of Orleans. Because I was genuinely interested in the girl and wanted to know what solution, if any, she could propose for troubled Ireland, I watched her on T.V. and listened sympathetically. Once again, I found myself listening to sound and fury signifying nothing, empty rhetoric, evasiveness, and not one single word of practical common sense. If a middle-aged man had come to Westminster and talked so, he would have been laughed at, yet because she was a girl she was hailed as a cross between Catherine na Houlihan and the Delphic Oracle.

185

Of course, it goes without saying that nearly all this publicity is given to the loud-mouths, the dissidents, the mavericks, however trivial, violent and evil their views and actions may be. In fact, the whole tendency of Press and T.V., especially the latter, is towards the sensational.

One really cannot blame the demonstrators, be they striking teachers or 'Stop-the-Seventy-Tour' boys, because it is becoming increasingly obvious that the easiest way to publicize one's cause is to create a disturbance. If you can get yourself arrested for shouting insults at a judge or for trying to burn down an Embassy, you have really got it made. Immediately, you are courted by interviewers, all with cameras, eager to present you with a ready-made audience of millions before whom you may parrot your slogans or air your grievance. If what you have to say is outlandish, and preferably obscene, you may be absolutely sure of all the publicity you could possibly hope for.

This positive encouragement by the mass media of everything to do with the young and, in addition, this addiction to sensationalism are a most dangerous combination, wholly inimical not only to the healthy development of the young themselves but even to our society as a whole. Nothing but evil can come from a growing conviction in the minds of the electorate that democratic methods and reasoned debate can achieve nothing, and that the only way to get things done is by establishing mob rule.

It is unfortunately true, as I have said before, that the ordinary voter seems to have less and less control over his own destiny and no means of making his influence felt with his masters. Time and again, he is faced with a *fait accompli* which he actively dislikes but is told that there is no arguing about it: for instance, decimalization, British Standard Time, the abolition of the death penalty, the closure of railways, compulsory-purchase orders, even entry into the Common Market. Vast numbers of people are bitterly opposed to all these measures but are absolutely powerless to influence decisions which, when once made, seem to be irreversible.

I believe that it would be a desperately dangerous thing if, at a time when people are suffering from the frustration of feeling themselves enslaved by a bureaucratic machine, it should become increasingly obvious that a determined and violent body of opinion, even when in a minority, can carry all before it and even impose its will on the majority. It is not too fanciful to see in this situation the state of mind that ultimately accepts political domination by a fanatical and ruthless minority party, whether it be of the Right or the Left.

I am quite prepared to face charges of oversensationalizing the issue, but I do not believe that I have done so. All these people who are making the headlines, especially the young, are from minority groups whose views and actions are being inflated beyond all reason by the amount of attention they get from the mass media. If we are to get back a sense of proportion and cut these young bullfrogs down to size, then it is imperative that the spotlight be turned off them, once and for all, both individually and in their mass demonstrations. We are rapidly reaching the stage when there is no such thing as a peaceful protest, for the whole process of demonstration makes mischief and breeds violence. Here again, I am going to stick my neck out and say that I think it might even be worth trying the experiment of forbidding all public demonstrations for six months, except within strictly limited bounds. For instance, why not set aside special places—Hampstead Heath, Newcastle Town Moor, the local football stadium or any other open space—and allow the protesters to assemble there and march about to their hearts' content with their banners and slogans? The demo could be advertised beforehand and anyone interested in what the protesters were likely to say could go along and watch and listen. A good time would be had by all and the ordinary public who do not want their Saturday-afternoon shopping disrupted by the banner-wavers and the slogan-shouters would be left in peace.

I can feel nothing but sympathy for the writer to *The Times* who complained bitterly that he and his wife and family were held up in their car for some considerable time while a protest march slouched past, in the main shopping-area of London. To make matters worse, as they sat there fretting and fuming, one of the marchers took some sharp instrument (a knife?) and scored deeply right along the side of the car as he went by, doing damage which cost a considerable sum of money to repair. Nothing could have more clearly demonstrated that the young man involved cared nothing at all for the particular cause he was allegedly supporting but was actuated by a blind hatred of anyone who owned anything which he coveted, in this case a car.

I am reminded of the time when I was driving in the general direction of Harwich and was flagged by two young people waving a banner with a strange device, the letters Y.U. I had an odd instinct about this and stopped, offering them a lift on condition that I was wrong about the meaning of their slogan. I was not: it meant, in effect, 'Why should you have a car when I have to walk?' as they admitted. So I told them to work damned hard and save their money, as I had done, and then they would be able to buy one. And I drove on.

This suggestion of limited demonstrations is not entirely frivolous, for one of the funniest demos I ever heard of was on the occasion when the Army played the Springbok rugby tourists at Aldershot. With true military efficiency and foresight the Army had marked out an empty field far enough away from the sports ground to leave the game undisturbed. They had posted notices *To the demonstration*, and even had soldiers unobtrusively directing the crowds in the right direction. As peaceful as a flock of sheep the protesters trooped along to the field and, almost before anyone realized what had happened, found themselves demonstrating away like crazy with no one taking a bit of notice. Of course, in this extraordinary democracy of ours whose freedoms seem daily more illusory than real, there would be an even greater howl going up if the sacred right of demonstration were interfered with than if someone actually did something to prevent near-pornography being peddled by the television networks. All I know is that if democracy means loading the revolver for the man who is going to shoot me dead, I am no democrat. Actively to encourage by every kind of publicity, co-ordinated disruption of everything that democracy has achieved over centuries, by those who boast of their settled hostility to that democracy and who seek to infect more and more of the young with their own nihilism and anarchism is irresponsibility bordering on lunacy. Let us recognize the threat for what it is before it is too late and the loaded revolver is pointing at our heart. It will matter little that the teenager who pulls the trigger is mouthing splendid slogans about the brotherhood of man; freedom will be just as dead as if he were chanting the 'Horst Wessel Lied'.

This then is what we must work for in all sectors of public life, if we are to align ourselves with the decent majority instead of allowing ourselves to be persuaded that the frenetic, alienated minority are typical and even admirable. We need, we badly need a lead from men in public life, be they politicians or churchmen. It is difficult to imagine anything more beastly, outside of the concentration camps of Nazi Germany, than the news which greeted us recently, that a side-effect of the well-intentioned Abortion Bill has been that living aborted foetuses have been sold by clinics to specialists for medical research. We learn that the intention was to try to keep these hapless creatures—for God help us all! they *are* creatures, living human beings—alive by artificial means until the full term of gestation, until in fact they were recognizable *babies*. Then they were to have been destroyed and used for some sort of medical research. To make matters worse, there has been a letter in *The Times* from a woman doctor, justifying this appalling experiment and saying: 'If the human foetus *which at present is readily available* [my italics] can be used for work which is to be applied to human beings it would be illogical to use an animal substitute.'

So indeed must the monsters have argued who used Jewish children for their hideous research during the war. They too were 'readily available', to the eternal shame and sorrow of humanity. What kind of a nation have we become where such things can happen, not in Dachau and Buchenwald but in 'swinging London', which once was called 'the floure of cities alle'?

Whether or not our leaders have the guts to make a stand against disorder and corruption, is it so impossible that in communications, in the arts, there may still be some men who are not drenched and impregnated with erotic obsessions and

189

are prepared to take positive action to resist atheism, immorality and lawlessness? Past civilizations have been destroyed by barbarians from without, but we are doing the job ourselves. We breed our own barbarians at the public expense, and our writers and newsmen faithfully chronicle their moral rottenness and hold it up for admiration. The second nastiest thing in the week's news as I write this chapter has undoubtedly been the sentimental slobbering of the Press over two squalid traitors, Ethel Gee and Harry Houghton. Every newspaper, with the honourable exceptions of the *Sun* and *The Times*, has considered their dreary 'love-life' of paramount importance and given them front-page coverage, ousting Cambodia, the financial crisis here and in America, and the General Election from the headlines. Two other news items illustrate further the irresponsibility of the people who have the power to shape public opinion: a literary critic reviewing a new book about the Royal Family barely conceals his contempt of them for being 'dull, married, straight, middle-class'. Is one to assume that the public figures he prefers are swinging, adulterous, kinky and working-class? (Let me add that, although I do not consider 'dull, married, straight' to be particularly pejorative terms, they admirably fit most of the working class of this country, who are probably the most conventional and respectable people alive.) The second item: a publishing-house, once well known for its rectitude and with a particular reputation for publishing religious books, has so far forgotten itself as to market yet another attack on the Christian faith by John Allegro. Quite apart from the fact that this book seeks to cash in on all the current obsessions by trying to equate the early Christians with some imaginary, drug-crazed, sex-obsessed tribe which, as far as I can see, never existed except in the author's imagination, it is a thoroughly bad and unscholarly piece of special pleading and one wonders why the publishers should have lent their imprint to it, except, of course, that it is likely to make money.

A third news item which fills me with bewildered despair rather than disgust is that a six-foot-high painting by Andy Warhol of a Campbell's soup-tin with peeling label—condensed vegetable beef soup if anyone is interested—has just fetched

£25,000 at a New York sale. It is a faithful, realistic representation which any competent third-former in secondary school could produce in an hour or so. It is also rather ugly and totally devoid of any merit, artistic or otherwise. And it has been offered for sale by reputable dealers, who have not scrupled to take £25,000 for this piece of trash.

I have quoted already from the Apostle Paul's letter to the people of Philippi and make no apology for doing so a second time; in fact, in all sincerity, I recommend it to the shapers of public taste and opinion as worthy of their serious consideration. Paul was accused of turning the world upside down because he castigated the corruption of the times and urged men in these terms: 'Whatever things are true, whatever things are of serious concern, whatever things are righteous, whatever things are chaste, whatever things are lovable, whatever things are well spoken of, whatever virtue there is and whatever praise-worthy things there are, consider these things.' I am not asking for hot-gospelling or a religious revival but merely for a recognition on the part of everyone in public life or at work in the creative arts, from politicians and newsmen to writers and painters, that there are other things worthy of consideration besides the torn labels of soup-tins, rescued from the trash-can.

Let us bring our children into the presence of greatness, instead of holding up to them as an example all that is lowest and most degraded in our society; let us show them beauty not only in the visible world but in human relationships, rather than expose them continually to the ugliness of life; let us show them love in all its loveliness instead of incessant propaganda which degrades human beings, and women in particular, into mere sex-machines which are cast upon the garbage-heap when old or worn out. If all we can do is show them a world where violence, lust, hatred and confusion reign, with no hint that there is anything better, how are they going to face the challenge of the future? They have before them the choice which Moses once put before the Israelites: 'I call heaven and earth to record this day against you, that I have set before you life and death, blessing and cursing, therefore choose life.'

What their choice will be depends on us.

13

To Strive . . . and not to Yield

There is no escaping the fact that the prime responsibility for the bringing-up of children rests with the parents, and, no matter what is done at school, by the church and by society in general, if the parents fall down on the job the chances of the child growing up into a happy and responsible adult are considerably diminished. I realize that in talking of children in the home, I am laying myself open to the charge of not knowing what I am talking about for I have no children of my own and have never had personal experience of the stresses and strains that exist within a family. Nevertheless, I have spent almost a professional lifetime with other people's children and all too often have had to salvage the wrecks that parents have made of their own children. Just as it is not essential for a doctor to have had measles himself in order to diagnose and treat it, so I do not think that the fact of not having biologically borne children renders one incapable of knowing how children should be treated by their parents. We have all known men and women who, though childless, would have made incomparably better parents than some of those who have actually produced children. I certainly make no such claim for myself and I have not the slightest idea what sort of a mother I should have made. I like to think that I might not have committed the grosser crimes against children which I have come across, nor perpetrated the worst stupidities.

It goes without saying that children from the moment they are born need love—inexhaustible, patient and unwearied—and they are going to demand a very great deal of their parents' time. When I was young my parents had some friends who were childless and who never ceased to lament the fact. I have a vivid recollection of the wife once saying to my mother that she would have given twenty years of her life to have had a child. My mother answered that twenty years of one's life was exactly what one had to give to a child. Quite frankly, if parents are not prepared to devote twenty years or more of their life to the bringing-up of their children, as my mother told her childless friend, then they simply should not have them at all. It seems very strange to me that although taking responsibility for the making of a new life and for moulding a character and personality is the most solemn and serious undertaking that anyone can face, it is nevertheless the one which is usually undertaken almost, if not entirely, by accident. When I was headmistress of a very large day school where many of the staff were young married women, I lost a lot of my romantic illusions about the sanctity of motherhood, if indeed I ever had any. Most of the young women whom one appointed to posts (during their last term at the university) were engaged when they came for interview and married when they joined the staff in September. Always, they assured one that they had no intention of having a child for several years, since their husbands were sometimes still at university, studying for higher degrees. Usually, they were living in a small flat or furnished rooms or even with their parents, and, of course, where there were two salaries going into the house, they were living up to every penny, running a car, buying furniture and other things on hire-purchase. Almost inevitably, they came during their first year to say that they were pregnant and would have to resign. The actual record was held by a young woman who came with this news at the autumn half-term. Of course, although one's heart sank at the prospect of yet another staff change, one murmured the customary congratulations. I have never quite got over the shock of being answered bitterly by one young woman, 'Well, it's nice that *somebody's* glad!'

The plain fact is that far too many unwanted children are born, and I do not mean out of wedlock. The old-fashioned idea of waiting until the bridegroom could make a home for his bride and afford to keep both her and the children when they arrived has been superseded ever since the war by the two-salary household burdened from the outset by a load of debt and an insatiable appetite for consumer goods. The wife has no intention of giving up her job on marriage, and, indeed, her wage is very necessary to them both, the family budget being calculated on what they both earn. When the children come, although I am sure that they are loved, the fact remains that they are an obstacle preventing the achievement of that standard of living on which the marriage has been based. As soon as ever possible, mother goes back to work, either full or part-time, often justifying her action to herself by saying that she is really doing it for the children. I do not pretend to know the solution to this problem because I can perfectly well understand the feelings of frustration of women cooped up at home all day with no company but small children, and also the difficulties of running a home for three or more people on one wage, where formerly there had been two wages for only two people. But this seems to resolve itself into the old question of privilege and responsibility or of not being able to have your cake and eat it too. If people want to be free and to enjoy the 'privileges' of being single, then they ought not to get married and have children, because you cannot have it both ways. Being married means always having to consider someone else as well as, even before, yourself. You can no longer 'enjoy' the selfishness of the unshared life. As soon as there are children, their interests must almost inevitably come first, before those of either of the parents. By this I obviously do not mean that their whims and fancies must be allowed selfishly to dominate the parents' lives but rather that their well-being must at all times and in all circumstances be the over-riding factor, for it is the parents who are responsible for the children and not the other way round. If ever parents adopt a course of action to suit themselves, without first considering most carefully the possible effects on the children, then they are failing in their duty.

Immediately after coming down from the university, I spent a month teaching in a special open-air school for convalescent children and part of the time I had a class of infants. Even making allowance for the fact that I had no training for teaching infants and absolutely no experience in dealing with such little ones, I can truthfully say that I found that week the most nerve-racking and exhausting of my life, so my sympathy goes out to any young mother coping with a refractory toddler. Even so, I did manage, aged twenty-one and unmarried, to deal unaided with forty five-year-olds and even to teach them something, so it does sometimes occur to me that parents might make a better job than some of them do of bringing up one or two.

For discipline does not begin in the teens nor yet when the child goes to school; it simply has to start as soon as a baby is old enough to want his own way rather than yours. One only has to look around to see innumerable examples of 'spoilt' children who are going to cause headaches and heartaches before they are very much older. I was once on a bus, empty but for myself, when a young mother got on with a toddler of about two years. I am sure that she was probably tired after shopping, although she was not laden with parcels, as I particularly noticed. She lifted the child into the bus, and he immediately ran right to the back and scrambled on to the seat, muddy shoes and all, standing up to gaze out of the back window. Now I, in my unmarried ignorance, would have adopted one of two lines with that little boy. Since the bus was empty, I would probably have followed him to the back, sat down beside him and made him sit too, explaining that it was not nice to put muddy feet on the seat. If I had had some special reason for remaining in a front seat, which was what the mother did, I would have gone back and fetched him forward to me. She did neither. Instead, she shouted to him to come to her. He refused. She called him again and again he refused. After a third call and yet another refusal she settled down in her seat, lit a cigarette and left him where he was. Shortly after, the bus pulled up sharply at traffic-lights and the little boy was thrown quite violently backwards on to the floor, hurting himself considerably and frightening himself even more. He picked himself up and ran weeping to his mother, who slapped him viciously, shook him and called him a naughty boy. Admittedly, she was probably reacting more in fright than in anger, because he might have had a nasty accident, but it seemed to me a classic case of how not to discipline a small child. In the first place, she deliberately created an opportunity for disobedience by calling him to her rather than going to him; secondly, when he disobeyed, instead of fetching him from the back at the first refusal she first nagged him and

195

then gave him his own way; finally, when his disobedience had resulted in pain and fear and he had run to her for comfort, she rejected him. Of all the possible lines of action at each stage of this little drama, the mother seemed to adopt the most disastrous of them.

Another day, I was shopping in the supermarket and seemed to be following a young couple, middle-class and educated from their speech and appearance, with their child of about four or five. He was creating a fair amount of chaos on every shelf, picking things up, knocking tins to the floor, getting in the way of the laden trolleys and so on. The first question that occurred to me was why was it necessary for both parents to come shopping since it would have been so much easier for father to have stayed home with the child while mother got the groceries? However, they seemed unconcerned at the swathe their off-spring was cutting through the shop so I assumed they were quite happy. As we all reached the cash-desk, the family still just in front of me, Junior got his eye on the sweets displayed beside it, and helped himself to a large bar of chocolate. Father took it from him and said he was not to have it, whereupon he promptly grabbed it back again. Once more, I seemed to see the obvious solution to the immediate difficulty and that was for father to restore the chocolate to the shelf and lead Junior through the narrow passage to the other side of the cash-desk where there were no sweets, leaving mother to pay for the groceries and put them in her bag. He preferred to remain where he was, again taking the chocolate away from the child but leaving him still within arm's length of the shelf. This time, Junior was *not* pleased; he went red in the face, started to scream and stamp and grabbed for the chocolate yet again. Father prevented him forcibly and got kicked for his pains, so he then selected a smaller chocolate bar and offered this to his screaming son. The boy screamed all the louder and flung the smaller bar on the floor, still struggling to reach the large one. Need I say what happened? Father meekly picked up the small bar and gave the large one to the child, but telling him that he must not eat it until after lunch as it would spoil his appetite. Only then did he lead the child away from the source of temptation, and even before he had got him past the desk the little boy was stripping the paper off the chocolate and preparing to eat it there and then.

Incidentally, all the time this had been going on, the entire queue of laden shoppers was held up since mother had not been able to get to the desk because of the antics of her offspring. After they had gone, the woman behind me remarked pleasantly, 'If that one was mine, I'd *murder* him!' I felt that I knew what she meant.

One more example of this almost incredible giving in to small children by their parents in situations which could so easily have been (a) avoided or (b) if not avoided dealt with in a proper manner: I was sitting on a beach at a seaside resort in the north of England, near where the ponies and donkeys were tethered, ready for the children to ride. The ponies were quite big, and only the older children rode them, the little ones sensibly preferring the donkeys. A very small boy approached, led by the hand by his father, a strapping six-footer, who proceeded to lift the child on to a donkey. The boy hit him smartly on the nose and struggled until Father put him down then, little legs apart and fists on small hips in furious defiance, he shouted, 'A'am not ganna ride on one o' them bloody things, Aa want a bloody 'orse or nowt!'

I must admit that I had to struggle hard not to laugh because the situation had its funny side, but it was Father's reaction that staggered me. He turned to me, obviously bursting with pride and said fondly, 'And 'e's not fower 'til Christmas!' Of course, the boy got his 'bloody 'orse'. I have often wondered what that child was demanding—and getting—by the time he was fourteen, since he had learned so well how to get his own way before he was four.

I have laboured the point enough: from the earliest age, it seems to me, one must try to make a minimum of rules for a child to keep, preferring rather to avoid areas of conflict whenever possible; but once a rule has been made and you are sure that you are right, then it must be kept or, if it is broken wilfully, there should be some punishment. Above all, once you have said 'No', you must mean it, and to give in to defiance or, worst of all, to screams and kicks, is fatal. When I was a very young child, we were reasonably well-to-do for my father was Chief Engineer on a large oil-tanker. I had a lot of toys, many of them expensive, and I knew that, providing my mother thought that what I asked for was good for me, I would get it. I have never forgotten being in the park one day with my mother and seeing other children riding 'fairy cycles', which were just becoming popular. I asked my mother if I might have one. We left the park immediately, took the tram to town where she bought me a splendid cycle, and we walked all the way home with Mother pushing me, for I had not learned to ride. Yet, at the same time, I knew very well that if I had asked for a penny and Mother had thought it was not a good idea to give it to me, I would not have got it. I would not have resented this; neither would I have asked twice, because I knew that 'No' never meant 'Perhaps'.

This sort of discipline was to stand me in very good stead when, in the Thirties, my father was 'on the beach', like many more Merchant Navy officers, and we had to live for two years on what we had saved and then on the dole. I was still only a child, but when I asked for things and was told that I could not have them because there was no money it never occurred to me to sulk or rebel or persist in my demands. When I was refused something, there was always a reason and I accepted the refusal with a good grace, secure in my parents' love and in the certainty that they would share their last penny with me if it was for my good.

I am not trying to pretend that I was a horrible little angel child, nor that my parents were plaster saints. I had my share of original sin like any normal healthy youngster, and I was always pretty strong-minded and fond of my own way. There must have been plenty of battles in the early days—indeed, my mother used to tell me that there were—and she had the disadvantage of bringing me up without the permanent presence of my father, who was often absent for months at a time when his ship was out East. My mother often said that she was sure no child was ever smacked more than I was! The odd thing is that I have absolutely no recollection of ever having a hand laid on me by either of my parents. The only corporal punishment I ever remember was once when I was punished at my junior school. To this day, I do not know why I was 'strapped' any more than I did at the time, for I was not conscious of having committed any crime. I resented that punishment bitterly because I did not understand the reason for it and felt it to be unjust. In an odd sort of way, I suppose I must still resent it, otherwise why should I remember it so vividly after forty-five years? Yet of all the times that I must surely have been punished by my parents, I have no trace of a memory. My parents have been dead for many years. I loved and honoured them and shall never cease to miss them.

It has been a constant source of surprise to me in my years of dealing with adolescents how little some parents seem to know about their children, and how ready they are to blame anyone but themselves for their child's shortcomings. The favourite scapegoat, of course, is the school. Teachers struggling to discipline a wayward fourteen-year-old who quite clearly gets far more of her own way at home than she ever does at school are frequently told accusingly by parents that she was never any trouble before she went to 'that school'. It never seems to occur to them that, since their daughter went to 'that school', she has changed from a child to a woman, with all that this means in physical, emotional and mental upheaval. I sometimes think that some adults are quite incapable of thinking back to how it felt to be the age of their child. One of the best descriptions of adolescence that I ever heard came from a distinguished headmistress at a conference I once attended. This is what she said:

How many of us recall what it felt like to be fourteen, an age when like Alice after she drank the medicine, you alternate between being ten inches high and a creature nine feet tall, demanding at one moment to be mothered and the next to be deferred to as a complete adult, and all the while shot through with that sensation of having fireworks inside your skin? Nowadays everyone has learned the jargon of sex and can chat superficially about deep, emotional things, but do we perhaps underestimate the real bewilderment of the child growing into adolescence? *We* look back and see the whole landscape as from a hill but *they* are down on the plain at the brambly entrance to the dark forest that the path runs through, and some of them are more afraid than they will admit. We can at least assure them that there *is* a path.

Even if we have never put a foot wrong in the upbringing of our small children, we can look out for squalls when the winds of adolescence begin to blow, and it is then that we need a double ration of love, understanding, tolerance, sympathy and, above all, patience. It is not the slightest use losing one's temper when a teenager answers, in reply to the question, 'Why did you do it?' with a simple but maddening 'I don't know'. This is nothing more nor less than the truth: the child does *not* know. It is at such time that a parent must bridle his tongue, take a deep breath, count ten and then set about trying to help the child to find out why, so that in the end he may understand himself a little better and be able to stand a little more firmly the next time the wind blows from that particular quarter. Parents (and for that matter teachers) must strive throughout the turbulent teens to make a child aware of his virtues and strengths as well as his faults and weaknesses and also to help him to recognize that many of his problems really will disappear as he gets older. Instead of an irritated 'I simply can't understand you', it might pay to say that we understand exactly how he is feeling because we went through it all at his age and we know how hellish life can be. However difficult it may be—and it is much more difficult for parent than for teacher to remain unemotional— we must try to preserve a kind of breakwater of compassionate imperviousness, against which the storms of adolescence can batter without doing any damage, thus providing a harbour of security and certainty in which the child can grow up.

At the same time as we exercise our sympathy and understanding, we must not be afraid to stand up resolutely for what we believe to be right. I am absolutely positive that young people *want* us to have principles, if only so that we give them something to argue about and rebel against, to flex their developing muscles, so to speak. If there is one motto which I would commend to anyone having to deal with the young, it is 'Thus far and no further', because I believe it to be the key to proper discipline. They must know where they are with you, just how far you are prepared to let them go and when you will insist on calling a halt. They positively enjoy testing out your authority—but do not imagine that they actually *want* to beat you hands down. There is no fun in winning a match if the opponent does not even put up a fight.

Above all, we must not shrink from letting the young for whom we have responsibility know where we stand on the important issues of the day. It is our own fault if they think that we do not *care* about world peace, apartheid, pollution, poverty and starvation. Have we ever taken the trouble to talk to them, to tell them what we think? We are so terrified of seeming to dogmatize, of being called propagandists, that we say nothing at all and the young very understandably come to the conclusion that we have no convictions. What we must never do is simply shout them down or refuse to listen to them on the grounds that they are talking nonsense or that we have not time. The fact that more often than not they *will* be talking nonsense, or at least what seems to us like nonsense, is no reason at all for not giving them a hearing. Only if we are prepared to listen to them will they be prepared to talk to us. There will be no generation gap if the people on either side are ready to employ reasoned arguments rather than prejudiced opinions, and in this dialogue it is the adult who must take the initiative. If we are, as we claim, wiser, better informed, more mature, infinitely more experienced, better balanced than the young, then it is up to us to prove it by using our superior attributes in order to help them. They certainly cannot help themselves or each other so who else can they turn to but us? It does not matter that, as often as not, they will seem to refuse our help: we must still continue to offer it. We must *never* reject them, however often they may reject us.

Some while ago, the viewing public was shocked by a T.V. film called *Gale is Dead*, all the more so because, some little time earlier, they had seen Gale, a heroin addict, very much alive, even though a sick girl with little hope of a future. What emerged most painfully from that film was that the real reason why Gale had died was because there was absolutely nobody in the world who cared sufficiently to want to keep her alive, and she knew it. Even those who knew her and were genuinely concerned for her could not spare sufficient time from their other pressing concerns to give her the attention and the love which she so desperately needed. Because here is the key to the whole problem of the successful development of the young. Granted there must be higher standards in those influences which have such a powerful pull on the teenager—T.V., films, books, theatre, advertising, all the things which I have tried to analyse in the foregoing chapters, but above all what is needed are *people*—people with enough concern and enough *time*. Schools, youth clubs, youth organizations, the churches, ministries of this, that and the other, can all play an important part, but first and foremost the most important person of all is the parent and it is the parent more than anyone else who seems to have opted out.

There are posters up in the local public library showing young children in potentially dangerous situations, situations which could easily lead to delinquency. The caption reads: *Do* you *know where your child is?* I should like to see that question on every hoarding throughout the length and breadth of the country. Do you know? Do you care? Or is it too much trouble to take time off from your own affairs to find out?

When I told an acquaintance that I was writing a book, I got the inevitable answer: 'I should love to write a book if only I had the time,' the maddening assumption being that she was so much busier than I and that that was the only reason why she did not produce a stream of immediate best-sellers. There is no polite answer to this remarkably silly statement, the plain fact being that there is always time for the things which one wants sufficiently to do. Surely, for us of the older generation there can be no task more immediate nor of more overwhelming importance than that of helping our young people to build up their future—all *our* future, as I have said. It is no easy task, nor is it one for weaklings, for the impatient, for the bigot or the hypocrite. Those of us who undertake it will be derided by some and impeded by many. The troubled state of the world and the waning power of our own country, the undermining of all the old authorities and the general debasement of standards are all powerful enemies whose strength we must not underestimate if we are to fight them. I shall never believe that we are fighting a losing battle because the majority are still on our side. It is not yet too late but it is nevertheless always later than we think and we have no time to lose.

I know that I shall be dismissed by some critics as so old-fashioned in my funny belief in goodness as to be entirely negligible. I do not think that I particularly care, so long as there are some people who may perhaps take courage and comfort from what I have written and re-enter the lists with renewed strength. Just so that my critics may have final and incontrovertible proof of my squareness, I am going to refer those who like myself have not given up hope to a writer incomparably greater but, if anything, squarer than myself, who wrote thus:

> . . . Come, my friends,
> 'Tis not too late to seek a newer world. . . .
> Tho' much is taken, much abides; and tho'
> We are not now that strength which in old days
> Moved earth and heaven; that which we are, we are. . .
> Made weak by time and fate, but strong in will
> To strive, to seek, to find, and not to yield.

Appendix

ADDRESS GIVEN TO FELIXSTOWE ROTARY CLUB, 5 MARCH 1970

When I was first asked to talk to you today, I believe I was asked what the subject was likely to be. To be quite truthful, that was so long ago that I have quite forgotten what I chose for my subject; but whatever it was, I have now changed my mind, which is, after all, a feminine privilege. Gentlemen, my subject today is a dirty word—though not spelt, I hasten to assure you, with the fashionable four letters. It has ten letters: D-I-S-C-I-P-L-I-N-E—discipline.

Now, I am well aware that by daring even to think about such an old-fasioned concept, I am branding myself as hopelessly square, utterly without it, and probably a repressed spinster to boot. Everyone seems to think that the revolt of the young against authority is the result of too rigid discipline in their formative years. I believe this to be utter nonsense, for this is the generation that has not been disciplined, that has never *met* the challenge of adult authority and is therefore being driven to one extreme after another, almost as though they were daring adults to stand up to them.

Is it not perhaps significant that when, some while ago, some students attempted a sit-in in the House of Commons, their protest collapsed as soon as the police appeared, and that leaders of some other student antics very quickly got out from under when writs were served on them? They did not, they said, want to go to prison. How very unheroic are these leaders of the revolution, when it comes to the push. I don't think that their dead hero Che Guevara would have had much use for them, if the mere thought of a short spell in the nick puts them off. I am therefore going to state quite unashamedly that it is my opinion that we are now reaping the bitter harvest of the permissive society, and that it is high time that those of us who refuse to be brainwashed into the belief that all truth, honour, nobility, not to mention might, majesty, dominion and power lie in the under-twenties stood up and said so.

I am sick and tired of listening to people of the older generation pouring out adulatory slush about the Young, who, we are told, are far, far better than ever we were at their age. Why are so many of us afraid to say what we think, to admit that we find most of their music a horrible row, instead of hailing the Beatles as the greatest song writers since Schubert, to state firmly that their dancing often resembles the twitchings of an epileptic and calls for neither grace nor skill, that their clothes are too often cheap and nasty rubbish, their hair-styles, both male and female, frequently hideous and that many of them could do with a good wash?

When I watch my contemporaries licking the boots of the teenagers, it amazes me that so many of the latter are the decent and charming young people that they are. John Lennon and Mick Jagger are held up for our admiration, not only because they have been convicted of possessing drugs but also because they got their girl friends pregnant. Middle-aged critics write lyrical praise of a play which exploits every possible aspect of sex and where every other word is an obscenity, because they apparently dare not admit that they really found the whole thing revolting and a bore into the bargain. Elderly dons come out—or should it be sit in?—in sympathy with striking students, much to the annoyance of the students, who wouldn't want to be found dead in the same sit-in as their elders. Ageing M.P.s write to *The Times* urging legalization of marijuana or the utter harmlessness of L.S.D., not because *they* want to turn on but because they feel it incumbent upon them to urge the young to do so.

I sometimes think that a rather nasty vicarious pleasure is at the root of a lot of this egging-on of the young to do the things which their elders never thought of doing. Most of us had a perfectly happy childhood and grew up quite unresentful of the discipline which our parents imposed on us. A misfit minority were unhappy and it is they who are urging young people to jump into bed with one another, to rebel, to wear outrageous clothes, to take drugs: in short, to do all the things which these sad, middle-aged, frustrated people imagine that they would have liked to do when they were young. And an equally misfit minority of the young takes this poisonous advice and, because they are noisy and exhibitionist, they are regarded as typical of their generation and pressure is brought to bear on the law-abiding majority to follow them.

Let me give you an example: a Sunday paper published a very useful page of advice to eighteen-year-old girls going to college or to a job for the first time. Mainly it was advice on budgeting, how much money to put aside for nylons, for cosmetics, for hair-dos, etcetera. Quite casually, and as though it were the most normal and natural thing in the world, one other item figured among the teenage expenses, so much a year for the contraceptive Pill. Gentlemen, am I being old-fashioned in thinking that one should not take it as normal and natural that an eighteen-year-old, away from home for the first time is automatically going to need the Pill? I maintain that, as it has ever been, a minority will sleep around at the earliest opportunity but the majority will not do so unless—and this is the crux of the matter—unless they are made to think, by articles such as this that I have quoted, that they are in some way unnatural or else a sexual failure if they do not.

To give you another example, I greatly enjoy the books of a certain best-selling novelist—and when I say best-selling, I am talking in terms of millions of copies all over the world. All this writer's women readers complain that as soon as a new book comes into the house it is grabbed first by the husband and then by all the teenage children, among whom there is a terrific following. Yet there is always some critic who, in reviewing these books, sneers at the decency of the characters because they do not find it necessary to jump into bed on the third page. Only the other day, one such critic wonderingly remarked that although the standards which this writer believes in are fast disappearing, millions of readers don't think that they are and continue to enjoy such books. Can it possibly be that the millions are right and the critic wrong?

I said that I was going to talk about discipline, and you may be wondering what all this has to do with my subject. Simply this: discipline is the teaching of standards—after all it comes from the Latin verb 'to learn'. It has nothing to do with corporal punishment, the writing of lines, detentions and all the petty punishments of certain schools, now, thank goodness, few and far between. It is useless to prate of self-discipline as if a baby were born knowing it. Self-discipline is the ultimate end of discipline but it cannot be achieved without guidance. Any community has the right to ask its members to develop within the framework of discipline which is the logical necessity of the community's existence. And, quite clearly, freedom to develop is quite different from freedom to do as you like. If one accepts the privileges and the protection of a community, be it a family, a school, a university or even a darts club, then one must accept the rules of that community.

Here I may be sticking my neck out but I am going to say quite categorically that I flatly deny the right of anyone who is still at the stage of taking from and not of giving to the community, to dictate to those who are the creators of the community what the rules should be. If students at a particular university do not like its rules, then my answer is: no one asked you to come here, you are here on money which you have not earned, there are thousands of young people who would give anything to be where you are now. So, if you don't like it, get out and get a job in a factory or, if that is beneath your dignity, then starve, because the community which you despise and which you are doing your best to destroy is not prepared to feed and clothe and house you any longer.

I have been in charge of teenage girls for twenty years, first as Deputy Head of a co-ed school and then as a headmistress. My basic attitude to discipline has not changed in those years because, though one varies the letter of the law, it is the same spirit which one interprets to different generations. When a girl questions an order, I always make it abundantly clear that *in the first place*, she obeys it because I say so and if she wants the kind of education which my school gives, then she accepts my authority. Nevertheless, I then see that she fully understands the reason for the rule which she is questioning, and I am always prepared to discuss it with her and even to change the rule if she can convince me that she is right and I am wrong. If anyone is shocked by my insistence that I'm the boss, all I can say is that it works.

Young people today are apparently so self-assured but underneath there is great uncertainty and they are almost tragic in their vulnerability, exposed as they are to the twin onslaughts of materialism and commercial exploitation. What they need is to be in touch with an imperturbable adult who is not easily pushed off balance or emotionally disturbed, against whom in the anxious years their storms can break and break again. They do not want to be left to make their own decisions before they have the mental and emotional maturity to do so. Every child should take responsibility as young as possible, but it must be measured to his capacity, enough to stretch him, but not too much, so as to become burdensome or oppressive. Even at the cost of family quarrels, he should never be left alone to make decisions which his parents believe will be harmful to him. Because once an adult adopts the policy of giving the child all he wants, where does it stop?

One thing you may be sure of, his demands will become more and more outrageous for the very reason that he is daring you to say no to him. And don't expect logic or sweet reason from an adolescent. Your teenage daughter is quite likely to upbraid you bitterly for insisting that she be in at what you call a reasonable hour, but she is equally likely to burst into floods of tears and say you don't care what happens to her if you say that she can stay out all night.

Which brings me to the most important point about discipline: that it must be rooted and grounded in love. Children must *know* that you care about them and that it is because you care that you are not going to allow them to run into danger. I could give you so many examples: the boy who once said that to live without rules would be like living in a quicksand; the weeping girl who, when her mother asked her what she wanted to do, wailed in despair, 'I don't want you to ask me, I want you to tell me'; the senior girl from a school where, because of a change of Head, discipline had become very slack, who said to me, 'It's horrible. We feel as if nobody cares what we do.' Of course, no child should be bullied or beaten, or at the other extreme over-protected, but so long as he is dependent for food, shelter, clothing, education—in short, for everything—on his parents and teachers, then I firmly believe that he does as they tell him. Parents' responsibility is to see that he knows why they tell him so, and if there is a mutual trust, love and respect he will accept this situation.

We do the young a grave disservice when we abdicate from judgement. For the children's sake, let us realize that adolescence is a most unstable age, both physically and emotionally, and that the bewilderment of the young is an appeal to us for values. The teenager is bombarded on all sides with pernicious propaganda which assures him that all his age-group like this and dislike that, wear certain clothes and do their hair a certain way, and that if he is different, if he is not with it, then he is somehow abnormal. This slavish adherence to group opinion is a most serious threat to the development of personality, and parents and teachers must help children to resist these pressures. But how can we do it? Certainly not by giving in to the black-mailing cry of 'Everybody else does it', nor by repeating 'I only want him to be happy' with its dangerous corollary 'Give him everything he wants'. Those parents who make a stand for what they believe to be right sometimes feel that they are fighting a losing battle. I do not believe that they are, but is it not better to light one candle than to sit and grumble at the darkness? Let our children be aware of our love and concern for them, not by the lavishness of the gifts we shower upon them, nor by the freedom to please themselves which we give them, but by the exercise of a kind but firm authority which will protect them from their own follies. Shakespeare was not far wrong when he said in *Antony and Cleopatra*:

> We, ignorant of ourselves,
> Beg often our own harms, which the wise powers
> Deny us for our good: so find we profit
> By losing of our prayers.

And finally, let us not be afraid to stand up to the noisy minority who would like us to believe that anyone over thirty is fit only for an old people's home. Let us say in no uncertain terms, 'This is *our* world, imperfect though it certainly is, we sweated and worked to build it, if some of us had not starved in the Thirties and if our friends and brothers had not died in the Forties, it would have been a hell of a lot worse world than it is.' Let us tell the young: 'For hundreds of years, the youth of Britain, when they reached your age, were slaughtered in their tens of thousands, and yours is the first generation to grow up to manhood and find a job waiting rather than a war. So give us some credit for keeping you alive at least. And we shall be very interested to see, when it is your turn to sweat and work and build, whether you do any better than we have done. Somehow we doubt it, but we wish you all the luck in the world. You'll need it.'